HERITAGE UNLOCKED
Guide to free sites in Yorkshire and the North East

Wheeldale Roman Road,
North Yorkshire

CONTENTS

As well as its many major attractions, such as Rievaulx Abbey and Lindisfarne Priory, northern England is home to many fascinating English Heritage sites to which entry is free. This book, one of a series of new guidebooks, provides a concise but informative introduction to each of these free sites.

The diversity of these sites reflects the long and varied history of this part of England. Among the earliest are the fortifications at Stanwick, demonstrating the power of the Brigantes tribe which controlled much of northern England before the arrival of the Romans in AD 43. Hadrian's Wall, the most important Roman monument in Britain, marked the empire's northern frontier. The significance of the region's Christian heritage is embodied in Anglo-Saxon remains such as St Peter's Church, Barton-upon-Humber and St Paul's Monastery, Jarrow. Impressive ruins of later medieval abbeys and priories still dominate the landscape and the legacy of Border warfare is seen in the many castles and fortified manor houses. Later sites, such as Derwentcote Steel Furnace, reflect

Runswick Bay, North Yorkshire

northern England's status as a world-leader in industrial innovation and enterprise. At St Mary's Church, Studley Royal, William Burges created one of the most superb examples of High Victorian Gothic Revival architecture in England.

Throughout this book, special features highlight aspects of the history and character of the region. This guide aims to help visitors to explore, understand and enjoy some of the lesser-known but intriguing monuments in the care of English Heritage. The sites are described in alphabetical order within each county of Yorkshire and the Humber and the North East respectively. A brief guide to English Heritage's admission-charging sites in these areas is given at the end of the book.

WITHDRAWN

Yorkshire and the Humber comprises the area including the city of York, the historic counties of the North, East and West Ridings and North Lincolnshire. It is a region of breathtaking landscapes – the hills and dales of the North York Moors contrast with dramatic coastlines dotted with historic ports and fishing villages.

Before the arrival of the Romans much of this region was controlled by the tribe of the Brigantes. Evidence of their power and prosperity can be seen in the

remains of their stronghold at Stanwick, where the fortifications are nearly 6.5km (4 miles) long, and where luxury imported goods have also been found. Late Iron Age or Roman

enclosures, possibly farmsteads, have also been discovered along the route of Wade's Causeway, a section of which runs across Wheeldale Moor. Surviving masonry of a bridge at Piercebridge also reveals the sophistication of transport networks in the north of Roman Britain.

The Yorkshire landscape is dominated by Christian monuments. At Whitby, St Hild founded an abbey in AD 657 that became a religious centre of international renown. Further south, St Peter's at Barton-upon-Humber is one of the most important surviving examples of an Anglo-Saxon church. It was, though, the monasteries founded from the 12th century onwards that have left some of the most distinctive remains. The soaring ruins of Rievaulx Abbey, the foremost Cistercian monastery in Britain, are a testament to its former greatness. In Lincolnshire, Thornton Abbey was the

Left: York Minster
Opposite: Shipwreck at Saltwick Bay, North Yorkshire

richest house of the Augustinian Order and its monumental gatehouse is one of the grandest surviving examples in Europe.

Less imposing, but just as intriguing, are the shallow, grass-covered foundations of medieval peasant houses at the villages of Wharram Percy in North Yorkshire and Gainsthorpe in North Lincolnshire. These are only two of the 3,000 villages throughout Britain which were abandoned between the 11th and 18th centuries. During the Middle Ages Yorkshire also played a strategic role in political and dynastic power struggles. Spofforth Castle, for example, was the main stronghold of the Percy family until the late Middle Ages. During the Wars of the Roses it was burned down by the victorious Yorkists, the Percys having sided with the House of Lancaster.

The region has been a thriving centre of industry for centuries; among the most important industries have been textile and steel manufacture, mining, quarrying and fishing. It was in northern England that the Industrial Revolution began in the late 18th century. Towns such as Bradford, Huddersfield and Halifax began to prosper in the 19th century and the magnificent Victorian buildings of this era, many of which have now been carefully conserved and restored, bear witness to this period of rapid growth.

Roseberry Topping, North Yorkshire

Piercebridge
Roman Bridge

Stanwick Iron
Age Fortifications

Richmond Castle ● ○ Easby Abbey

Whitby Abbey ●

*Mount Grace
Priory*

Wheeldale
Roman Road

Middleham Castle ●

NORTH
YORKSHIRE

Rievaulx Abbey

*Pickering
Castle*

*Scarborough
Castle*

Marmion Tower ○

*Helmsley
Castle*

St Mary's Church,
Studley Royal

Byland Abbey

*Aldborough
Roman Site*

Wharram Percy
Deserted Medieval
Village

Fountains Abbey

Kirkham Priory

Burton Agnes
Manor House

Spofforth Castle ○

Clifford's Tower

Skipsea Castle

EAST RIDING OF
YORKSHIRE

Steeton Hall Gateway ○

Howden Minster

Thornton
Abbey &
Gatehouse

WEST YORKSHIRE

St Peter's Church

NORTH
LINCOLNSHIRE

N E
LINCS

*Brodsworth Hall
& Gardens*

Gainsthorpe
Medieval Village

Monk Bretton Priory

SOUTH
YORKSHIRE

*Conisbrough
Castle*

Roche Abbey ●

○ Unstaffed sites
● *Staffed sites*

7

History

The manor house, or Old Hall, at Burton Agnes was built by Roger de Stuteville between 1170 and 1180. The hall, like the village, was named after one of his daughters. In 1274 both passed by marriage to another notable family, the Somervilles. In about 1323 Joan Somerville married Rhys ap Gruffud. Their descendant Sir Walter Griffith is credited with restoring the Old Hall and adding its present roof in the 15th century. The

The south and east fronts of Burton Agnes Manor House, remodelled in the early 18th century

adjacent new Hall (not in the care of English Heritage, but open to the public) was built by Sir Henry Griffith between 1601 and 1610, probably to designs by Robert Smythson. In 1654 the estate passed to Sir Henry's nephew Sir Francis Boynton, and it remains in the ownership of the Boynton family.

In the early 18th century the Old Hall was partly rebuilt in brick and converted to a laundry. The new Hall was partly remodelled around the same period. The Old Hall was taken into guardianship in 1948 and a programme of restoration was undertaken, including the repair and remodelling of some of the original openings. Excavations were carried out at the site in 1984.

Description

The south and east facades, in brick with stone-framed sash windows, date from the early 18th-century remodelling. The building retains many of its original medieval features, however, which can be identified with ease. These features include the stone plinth, with blocks of limestone masonry above, in the west elevation, and in the north wall a restored ground-floor window, a large chimneybreast and a first-floor door, originally reached by an external stair. The string course at first-floor level dates from the 15th century. Although traditionally identified as the manorial hall, the building may have been a chamber block, used for the lord's private accommodation; in either case it is a rare and important survival of a late Norman building.

The undercroft of the manor house

The undercroft of the hall has an impressive vaulted ceiling supported by stout columns with simple carved capitals. This area provided storage space. The vault infill is of clunch, a type of chalk. Excavation of part of the brick floor revealed that the original floor was of rammed chalk. The pillar farthest from the door is scratched with a pattern of small holes set in rectangles. These may have been peg-holes for playing the game of 'nine men's morris'. In the north-east corner is the original 12th-century spiral staircase, lit by a small window. Nearby was an inserted 18th-century staircase, now removed.

The staircase leads up to the hall on the first floor, with a 15th-century roof. A second floor, added in the 18th century, has since been removed, although the windows to this upper storey remain. Behind the building is the wellhouse with its reconstructed 17th-century wheel, which would once have been turned by a donkey, to draw water from the medieval well.

In Burton Agnes village, 5 miles SW of Bridlington on A166
OS Map 101, ref TA 102632
Open
1 Apr–31 Oct:
11am–5pm daily

History

St Peter's Church at Howden was originally an Anglo-Saxon foundation. Following the Norman Conquest it was granted by William I to Durham Priory. In 1267, after a failed attempt to set up a monastic community, the Bishop of Durham made arrangements for the church to become collegiate, that is, served by a body, or college, of priests known as canons, who did not belong to a religious order. The church was endowed with six nearby parish churches – Howden, Barnby, Thorpe, Skelton, Saltmarsh and Skipwith – to provide income for the community.

In the 1270s the building of the new church began and by 1306–11 the west front was complete. Between 1320 and 1340 a new aisled choir was built. The ornate chapterhouse was constructed in two phases from the 1340s, its completion being funded by Walter Skirlaw, Bishop of Durham (1388–1406). Parts of Skirlaw's manor house still exist south-east of the church, now fronted by a later elegant

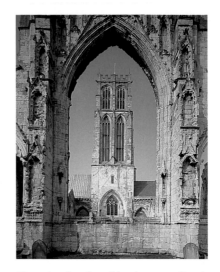

Georgian facade, with a large medieval moat and fishpond in the park beyond. In the late 15th century the minster's great landmark tower was completed. Although the collegiate church survived Henry VIII's Dissolution of the Monasteries it was suppressed by Edward VI in 1550. The town and church of Howden quickly fell into decline. The income of the church passed to the Crown and the maintenance of the building became the responsibility of the parishioners, who were obliged to abandon the choir through lack of funds for maintenance. In 1696 the great vaulted roof of the choir collapsed. The roof of the chapterhouse fell down in 1750. The ruined choir and chapterhouse were taken into guardianship in 1971 and the latter was repaired and reroofed in 1984.

Description

The site can generally be viewed from the outside only. Through the gate you can see the ruined choir of the church, later used as a graveyard. It had two aisles and the central portion stood three storeys high. The octagonal chapterhouse has traceried windows with arched canopies, and outer buttresses with decorative shields. Inside are elaborate carved stone panels above the stone benches where the canons sat for meetings. At the doorway between the choir and the chapterhouse is a tiny chapel, probably the one founded by Bishop Skirlaw in about 1404.

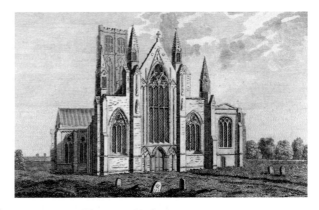

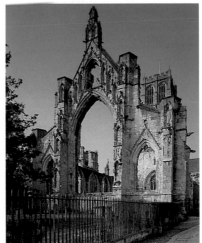

Above: Howden Minster in an 18th-century engraving

Left: The remains of the choir today

In Howden, near the junction of A63 and A614 OS Map 106, ref SE 748283

11

History

Skipsea Castle, a motte-and-bailey fortification constructed between 1071 and 1086 by Drogo de la Beauvrière, first Lord of Holderness, was one of the earliest castles to be built in Yorkshire after the Norman Conquest. It was the principal residence of the powerful Lords of Holderness until, some time before 1200, they moved near to their newly created (but ultimately short-lived) port on the Humber at Hedon. King Henry III ordered the defences to be slighted in 1221, although this order may never have been carried out, for the castle seems to have remained in use until about 1250. The medieval masonry was later dismantled for re-use elsewhere. Skipsea Mere (a lake occupying the surrounding low-lying ground) was also drained and fields were laid out over the bailey and ploughed, levelling part of the defences. The largest earthworks were allowed to decay gradually into grassy banks and mounds. The site, except the motte, came into state guardianship in 1911.

Motte-and-bailey castles of this type are not rare but Skipsea's conical motte appears to be exceptionally large. In fact, this is an illusion created by its carefully chosen location on a natural glacial mound. The marshy ground surrounding the motte is also natural, although recent research by English Heritage

Skipsea Castle's motte, built on top of a glacial mound

suggests that an earth dam (probably constructed at the same time as the castle) was added to trap more water, creating Skipsea Mere. This large, shallow lake would have served as a defence, as a fish pond and as an ornamental feature. The motte and bailey would have been vulnerable to attack from the higher ground and to guard against this, a borough, or defended town, known as Skipsea Brough like the modern settlement, was built on the top of the ridge. It was enclosed within a massive earth rampart which also encompassed the main through-route descending to the easiest crossing of the marshy ground. Today, it is difficult to understand why a castle was built in this apparently remote area. Evidently the route crossing the marsh must have been more important in the Middle Ages. The small coastal port that the Lords of Holderness tried to develop nearby failed to thrive and there is little evidence to suggest that the town on the ridge proved any more successful: there are few traces

of buildings. Ultimately, neither town nor castle was sufficiently well sited to encourage its continued use.

Description

Visitors approach through the gate and walk up to the brow of the ridge. The motte, surrounded by a low rampart, can be seen ahead to the north. The bailey was in front of this but parts of its defences are now difficult to distinguish as a result of later ploughing. The defensive bank that surrounded the borough, to the left, remains more obvious. The mere lay behind the motte and would have extended into the natural channel along the foot of the ridge, separating the borough from the bailey. A relatively recent cutting along the farm track leads through a mound which possibly marks the site of a gate tower. This would have been built to control access into the bailey. The main gate is thought to have faced south-east towards the church, with the main street of Skipsea aligned on it.

8 miles S of
Bridlington, W of
Skipsea village
*OS Map 107,
ref TA 162551*

13

History

The Premonstratensian abbey of Easby is set in picturesque surroundings beside the River Swale, close to the town of Richmond. According to late medieval authorities, Roald, Constable of Richmond Castle, founded the abbey in 1152. A community of priests may have already been established here in Anglo-Saxon times. The abbey's early history is obscure, but in the 14th century the Scrope family became its patrons. In 1392, following a grant of land by Sir Richard Scrope, the community was substantially enlarged. Numbers were sustained into the late 15th century but by the mid-1530s only 11 canons remained. Easby was dissolved in 1536 and within two years most of the buildings had been stripped of their lead roofing and partly demolished. Extensive and impressive ruins survived, however, and from the late 17th century they became a favourite subject for artists and, later, photographers. In 1792 Viscount Torrington wrote that 'there cannot be a more perfect ruin [or] a nicer ruin … or one of happier situation'.

Description

Today, visitors approach the abbey down a lane, passing on the left the splendid early 14th-century outer gatehouse, complete apart from its roof. It has a large doorway for vehicles and an adjacent smaller one for pedestrians. Within the monastic precinct, just across the lane from the gatehouse, is the parish church, with a remarkable surviving fragment of late 12th-century stained glass. Easby

The refectory on the south side of the cloister at Easby

was known as St Agatha's Abbey, after the dedication of the church. To find a parish church, used for public worship, within the precinct of a monastery is rare in England, but the Premonstratensians were not a closed order cut off from worldly contact. The monastic ruins are substantial, though, except for the north and south transepts, most of the church has been reduced to foundation level. There are, however, seven excellent examples of medieval grave slabs, incised with crosses and other decoration, and some areas of floor tiles also survive.

The plan of Easby is most unusual because of the limitations imposed by the site and by earlier buildings. The cloister ranges are well-preserved. On the east side is the chapterhouse – with stone benches for the monks built into the walls – and the remains of the parlour. Normally, the dormitory would have been above these, but at Easby it was in the west range, so that the adjacent latrines could be flushed by water brought in a subterranean drain from the river. The west range

Easby Abbey,
*by William Callow
(1812–1908)*

is a massive complex built into the slope towards the River Swale on three storeys. It comprises undercrofts, guest accommodation, storerooms, latrines and dormitories. These are all interconnected by passages, staircases and doorways. The finest buildings are on the south side of the cloister where the magnificent refectory, set above a large vaulted undercroft, stands to roof height. It has tall windows with delicate Gothic tracery. The other unusual feature at Easby is the substantial range of buildings on the north side of the church. Reached from the north transept, they include a complex of chambers that served as infirmary, abbot's lodging and chapel.

1 mile SE of
Richmond,
off B6271
OS Map 92,
ref NZ 185003
Open
1 Apr–30 Sep:
10am–6pm daily;
1–31 Oct:
10am–5pm daily;
1 Nov–31 March
10am–4pm daily

From the mid-7th century onwards, the seemingly bleak and inhospitable coasts, moors and dales of Yorkshire and the North East became fertile ground for the foundation of monastic communities. Among the earliest foundations were those established by St Aidan at Lindisfarne on Holy Island in 635 and by St Hild at Whitby in 657. Both were religious centres of great renown in the Anglo-Saxon world, Lindisfarne primarily as a centre for the cult of St Cuthbert.

Although these two monasteries were abandoned two centuries later, owing to Viking raids, their memory would inspire a great revival in monasticism following the Norman

Above: Opening page of St John's Gospel from the Lindisfarne Gospels

Left: The ruins of Rievaulx Abbey in North Yorkshire

Conquest of 1066. New Benedictine foundations – those observing the Rule of St Benedict – followed soon after William the Conqueror's infamous 'harrying of the north' in the winter of 1069. Great churches and monasteries demonstrated the power of the Norman elite as much as their castles.

It was the next generation of monasteries, many of which were established by the Augustinian and Cistercian orders, that had such a distinctive impact on the north. Cistercian monks adopted an ascetic discipline, renouncing rich ornaments, elaborate rituals, ownership of personal property and the consumption of meat. Within a few years of the foundation of the first Cistercian abbey in northern England, at Rievaulx in 1131, several communities had been created in Yorkshire and the North East. In these parts of England, Abbot Aelred of Rievaulx discerned 'everywhere serenity and a marvellous freedom from the tumult of the world'.

Norman landowners proved willing patrons and their gifts brought both spiritual and practical benefits. The monks' involvement in land improvement – creating farm estates and building roads and bridges, for example – had a major impact on the economy of the region. Unlike the Benedictines, the Cistercians exploited the land directly through *conversi*, lay brothers who lived a simple life of prayer and manual labour. By 1167 there were 140 choir monks and 500 *conversi* at Rievaulx. A system of granges and sheep lodges enabled the monks to administer extensive estates, and has left its mark on the topography of the region, evident, for example, in the villages that originated as monastic granges. The growth of market towns and ports was also fostered by monastic trade, especially in wool.

By 1200 almost every religious order was represented in the region, each with its distinctive traditions. Orders of canons, such as the Augustinians (at Brinkburn Priory and Thornton Abbey) and the Premonstratensians (at Easby Abbey and Egglestone Abbey), were all priests, sometimes ministering to the local district. In Yorkshire alone there were some 30 houses of nuns by 1200, though they were relatively poorly endowed and have left few standing remains. The friars, with their simple life of preaching and begging, were largely an urban phenomenon. By 1230, only a few years after the foundation of the two orders, there were Franciscan and Dominican friaries in York. Communities of Austin Friars and Carmelites soon followed there and elsewhere.

Reconstruction drawing of Easby Abbey in about 1500

After Mount Grace Priory, a Carthusian establishment, was founded in 1398, there were almost no new monastic foundations in Yorkshire and the North East before they were suppressed in 1536–9. The destruction of those years dealt a devastating blow to the region's economic life and to the religious outlook that underpinned it.

MARMION TOWER

History

West Tanfield is situated on the banks of the River Ure, where the main route from Ripon once crossed the river. A stone bridge, constructed by 1725, replaced the original ferry.

Located west of the bridge near the church of St Nicholas, Marmion Tower is the entrance to, and the only significant remaining part of, a former manorial complex. A residential gatehouse of this type is not unusual, but the quality of the accommodation in the upper two storeys – shown by the fine carving and detailing – makes the building distinctive. The rooms in the gatehouse might also have served as the private apartments to the manorial block.

The entry in Domesday Book records that the manor at West Tanfield was held in 1086 by Count Alan of Richmond Castle. The Marmion family owned the manor for much of the 13th and 14th centuries, but the

Marmion Tower, showing the striking oriel window on the first floor

gatehouse dates from the 15th century. It was probably built by William Fitz Hugh, who died in 1452.

After the death of his grandson's wife, the manor passed to the Parr family. Later alterations, in the 16th century, were probably made by William Parr, who was Marquis of Northampton and brother to Katherine Parr, the sixth wife of Henry VIII. The manor was granted to William Cecil, Lord Burghley, in 1571. Following later changes of ownership, the tower was placed in guardianship in 1976.

Description

The square tower is three storeys high with a vaulted gate passage set off centre. The different appearance of the masonry at second-floor level shows where the tower was heightened. The most striking feature on the east face is the fine oriel window at first-floor level.

The vaulted ceiling at the eastern end of the gate passage is higher than that at the opposite end; this allowed the gates to open inward. To the left is a small doorway leading into the porter's lodge. This room is vaulted, with a fireplace and a small opening for a cupboard in the south wall. A door leads to the garderobe (latrine) in the south-west corner. A small squint in the north wall enabled the porter to look into the passage.

A spiral staircase at the north-west corner of the gate passage leads up to the first floor. At the entrance to the first floor a recess has been cut into the west wall to allow the door to open. This is probably because the ground-floor vaults replaced an earlier timber floor set at a lower level.

The first-floor room has similar features to the ground-floor room, such as a garderobe and a fireplace, but these are more ornate. The elaborate oriel window replaced an earlier window recess. On the second floor a horizontal channel is visible along the wall. This carried the support for the floorboards and the earlier roof structure before the tower was heightened.

On A6108 in
West Tanfield
OS Map 99,
ref SE 268787
Open
1 Apr–30 Sep:
10am–6pm daily;
1–31 Oct:
10am–5pm daily;
1 Nov–31 Mar:
10am–4pm daily

PIERCEBRIDGE ROMAN BRIDGE

History

The Roman fort at Piercebridge was connected to the road now known as Dere Street. This road linked York with Corbridge on Hadrian's Wall, and incorporated two bridges over the River Tees. The earlier bridge, made entirely of timber, was washed away as the course of the river changed northwards, although parts of the structure still remain underwater. The second bridge, downstream of the first, was uncovered during quarrying in 1972–3. This bridge was built of wood but was supported by stone abutments and five masonry piers. During excavations a southern approach road was discovered, together with several buildings from the Romano-British settlement. Pottery from these buildings helped to date the construction of the bridge to possibly the 2nd or 3rd century AD. In the mid-4th century, as the river's course continued northwards, the southern abutment silted up and a metalled causeway with a retaining wall of cut limestone slabs was built over the top. A civilian settlement grew up around the fort, on both sides of the river, with the bridge connecting the two parts. Several Roman buildings, including a barrack block and a bath house, were revealed during excavations in the 1970s.

Fallen masonry, showing the positions of four out of five piers of Piercebridge Roman bridge

Description

Three components of the bridge have been discovered – the abutment at the south end, the pavement that consolidated the river bed and the masonry piers that carried the structure over the river. The southern abutment has a dressed stone surface with iron clamps. It stands 1.2m (4ft) high from the paved surface on the riverside and is level with the grass bank on the opposite side. Five holes, in which timber beams for the bridge superstructure were inserted, can be seen on the river side of the abutment. The pavement of sandstone blocks was laid on the river bed to prevent the river undermining the piers. Two gaps in the pavement and two piles of

fallen masonry show the position of four of the five piers, with that of the fifth being marked by stone in the grass bank. The northern abutment, not found in the excavations, was probably destroyed by river action. Part of the later causeway survives as a bank with a revetment of stone to the east of the pavement.

The position of the fifth pier, marked by stone set in the grass

Reconstruction giving an idea of the appearance of the bridge in Roman times

At Piercebridge, 4 miles W of Darlington, on B6275
OS Map 93, ref NZ 214155

21

St Mary's Church from the south-east
Facing page: *The richly painted chancel ceiling*
Below: *Winged lion sculpture inside the church*

History

St Mary's is set within the Studley Royal Estate, an 18th-century designed landscape that encompasses the magnificent ruins of Fountains Abbey, founded in 1132, and the famous water gardens. St Mary's, designed by the renowned architect William Burges for the first Marquess and Marchioness of Ripon, was built as the estate church. It is also a memorial to the marchioness's brother Frederick Vyner, who was kidnapped and held to ransom in 1870 while travelling in Greece. Before the money could be paid he was killed during a rescue attempt. Both St Mary's and its companion church, Christ the Consoler at nearby Skelton, were commissioned from Burges, and the unpaid ransom went towards their construction. The foundation stone of St Mary's church was laid in 1871 and the church was consecrated in 1878. Both the marquess and the marchioness are buried in the church and are commemorated by a sumptuous marble monument in the south-aisle chapel.

St Mary's ceased to be used for services in 1970 and passed into state guardianship. In 1986 the Studley Royal Estate, including the church and the abbey, was placed on the list of World Heritage Sites, as a man-made landscape of international historic and aesthetic significance.

Description

Burges skilfully integrated the new church into an existing setting. Situated in the north-west part of the estate, within the deer park, it forms the terminus of an axis that runs down the grand avenue of lime trees towards the west front of Ripon Cathedral. The large spire of St Mary's is prominent in the Studley Royal landscape and the view to Ripon from the church is breathtaking on a clear day.

Burges is best known for his domestic work for the Marquess of Bute at Cardiff Castle and Castell Coch in Wales. He travelled in France and Italy, sketching medieval Gothic buildings that inspired the romantic architectural style with which he is associated. St Mary's is considered by many to be his ecclesiastical masterpiece. It is one of the finest examples of High Victorian Gothic Revival architecture in England, designed by one of the style's most eminent proponents. Burges was concerned with all aspects of the design of the church, from the plan to the decorative details of the interior. He worked closely with a skilled team of craftsmen on the stained glass, wall paintings, mosaic floor, marble panelling and organ. Built of grey

limestone and with a grey slate roof, St Mary's Church is in an elaborate 13th-century Decorated Gothic style. It is adorned with richly carved sculpture, in particular round the west door

and the west window. Elaborate ironwork embellishes the wooden south and west doors. The interior features coloured stone and marbles, carved, painted and gilded details, and painted saints, angels, stars and symbols of Paradise lost and regained. The chancel is the visual and symbolic climax of the building. Its walls are lined with marble, outlined with mosaic and the ceiling is richly painted. The original plan to decorate the nave and aisles in the same way was never implemented, probably owing to costs.

2¹/₂ miles W of Ripon, off B6265; in the grounds of the Studley Royal Estate
OS Map 99, ref SE 275693
Open
1 Apr–30 Sep: 1–5pm daily
Tel: 01765 608888

The dramatic landscapes of Yorkshire and the North East have inspired generations of notable writers and artists, particularly from the 18th century onwards. Perhaps the best known novelists associated with Yorkshire are the Brontë sisters, Charlotte, Emily and Anne, who lived at Haworth in the Pennines in the first half of the 19th century. Charlotte's *Jane Eyre* and Emily's *Wuthering Heights*, both published in 1847, are among the best-known works of English literature. Whitby features in *Dracula*, one of the most famous works of horror fiction, published by Bram Stoker in 1897. In the novel, the count disembarks in the town, where he attacks his first English victim, Lucy Westenra.

In the 20th century the writers James Herriot and Catherine Cookson had worldwide success. Herriot's *All Creatures Great and Small* and other stories were inspired by his experiences as a veterinary surgeon in North Yorkshire in the 1940s and 1950s. Cookson found fame with her romantic yet realistic novels set in her native Tyneside. The illegitimate daughter of a servant, she wrote more than 40 books, telling the story of her own life in the 1969 novel *Our Kate*. At Scarborough in 1971, the playwright Alan Ayckbourn was appointed artistic director of the Stephen Joseph Theatre, where many of his plays have been premiered.

Andrew Marvell, one of the most renowned early Yorkshire poets and a writer of great wit and elegance, was born at Winestead in Holderness in 1621. He attended the grammar school in Hull and, a supporter of Oliver Cromwell, became an MP for the town in 1659. Three hundred years later Hull was also home to the poet Philip Larkin, for many years librarian at the university's Brynmor Jones Library. His poem *The Whitsun Weddings*, describing a train journey from northern England to London, epitomises his witty, wry style. Hull is still celebrated today for its poets, including Douglas Dunn and Peter

Above: The Brontë Sisters (c 1834), by their brother, Patrick Branwell Brontë

West View of Thornton Abbey *(c 1794), by Thomas Girtin*

Didsbury. Ted Hughes, Poet Laureate from 1984 until his death in 1998, was born in Mytholmroyd. As a child he roamed the hills around his birthplace and aspects of his work celebrate this landscape. In *Remains of Elmet* (1979), his poems accompany Fay Godwin's black-and-white photographs of the Calder Valley. Basil Bunting, born in Scotswood upon Tyne in 1900, was unknown until the publication of his long, semi-autobiographical Northumbrian poem *Briggflatts* in 1966.

In the late 18th century one of England's greatest artists, J M W Turner, toured and painted sites in northern England, as did the watercolourists John Sell Cotman and Thomas Girtin. Several notable 20th-century

Right: The Angel of the North *(1998), by Antony Gormley*

artists are natives of Yorkshire. Henry Moore, the son of a coalminer, was born in Castleford in 1898. His contemporary, Dame Barbara Hepworth, was born in Wakefield in 1903. Both are famous for their striking semi-abstract and abstract sculptures, now often exhibited in outdoor settings. The sculpture for which the North East is best known today is probably *The Angel of the North* (1998) by Antony Gormley. With a wingspan of 54m (175 ft) it stands guard over the A1 near Gateshead.

Born in Bradford in 1937, David Hockney trained in the town's School of Art and went on to produce work in a wide range of forms, especially painting, photography and stage design. He is especially celebrated for his 'California' paintings, but his most recent works include a series of East Yorkshire landscapes. A wide range of Hockney's works is now on permanent display at Salt's Mill, Saltaire, West Yorkshire.

History

From the Norman Conquest until the 17th century, Spofforth was in the possession of the Percy family, one of the most important and influential families in northern England. It was the principal Percy seat until the late 14th century. William de Percy, a favourite of William the Conqueror, built a manor house here in the 11th century, although nothing remains of this earlier building. Reputedly it was here that rebel barons drew up Magna Carta in 1215. In 1224 Henry III granted a licence to a later William de Percy to hold a Friday market in the town and in 1308 Henry de Percy received a licence to fortify the manor house.

During the Wars of the Roses the Percys supported the House of Lancaster. Following the battle of Towton in 1461 the victorious Yorkist side, led by the Earl of Warwick, marched on Spofforth, burning the castle and plundering the local countryside. The castle lay in ruins for nearly 100 years until 1559, when it was restored by Henry, Lord Percy. By this time, however, the seat of the Percys had shifted to Alnwick in Northumberland. The last recorded occupant was the castle steward Sampson Ingleby, who died in 1604. The castle was finally reduced to ruin during the Civil War. In 1924 Charles Henry, Baron Leconfield, transferred ownership of the site to the state by deed of gift.

Description

Spofforth Castle is situated on a small rocky outcrop overlooking the village. The medieval manor house was arranged around a courtyard but only the west range, which contained the principal apartments, still stands. Only

Facing page: Plan of the west range of Spofforth Castle

Spofforth's west range, the only part of the castle still standing today

earthworks and some low walls remain of the north, south and east ranges. A flight of steps leads down from the site of the courtyard to the ground floor of the west range. At the south end is the earliest part of the building, dating from the 13th century. The west range was built against the rocky outcrop. A passage cut directly through the rock led up to the great hall but was later blocked, probably in the 15th century. The remains of a row of columns and stone corbels on the west wall date from the 14th century, when a stone vault was added. At first-floor level the east and west walls were totally rebuilt during the 15th century with impressive windows in each wall.

At the far end of the undercroft the solar, or private chamber, is reached through a door in the north-west corner. The solar block, added in the 14th century, is very similar in design to that at Markenfield Hall, near Ripon, with a spiral stair turret leading from the main chamber up to the first floor. The door in the north-east corner leads into

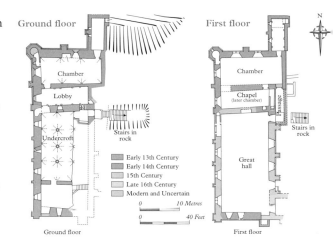

Ground floor

First floor

Chamber

Lobby

Chapel
(later chamber)

Undercroft

Passage

Stairs in
rock

Stairs in
rock

Great
hall

Early 13th Century
Early 14th Century
15th Century
Late 16th Century
Modern and Uncertain

0   10 Metres

0   40 Feet

Ground floor

First floor

the garderobe, or latrine tower. On the first floor a passage, now ruined, leading from a private chamber and chapel, gave access to the great hall. The great hall could also have been entered through a doorway at the south end of the east wall, where there would probably also have been a passage leading to the buttery and kitchen. The chapel has a finely moulded window in the west wall but was probably later converted to accommodation, a garderobe being added in the east wall.

3½ miles SE of
Harrogate, off
A661 at Spofforth
OS Map 104,
ref SE 360511
Open
1 Apr–30 Sep:
10am–6pm daily;
1 Oct–31 Mar:
10am–4pm daily

The features now visible at Stanwick are the excavated remains of only a small part of an Iron Age rampart and ditch that encloses an area of 310 hectares (766 acres) and is nearly 6.5km (4 miles) long. Excavations were conducted by the celebrated archaeologist Sir Mortimer Wheeler in the 1950s and the remains were left uncovered and partly reconstructed to show their original appearance. From these excavations Wheeler was able to date the rampart to the 1st century AD. The ditch was cut into the bedrock and the ramparts were reinforced with a retaining stone wall. It is thought that this wall ran around the full circuit of the outer rampart. It would have been a most impressive sight, and its construction would have required an enormous workforce. The ability to command such a force lay with the powerful local ruling class of the Brigantes who controlled much of northern Britain when the Romans arrived in AD 43. In exchange for their independence their queen, Cartimandua, agreed to co-operate with the Romans. The treaties were not accepted by the whole tribe, however, and a power struggle between the different factions followed.

The Brigantes' occupation of Stanwick was concentrated on the area known as the Tofts, to the south of the church of St John the Baptist. Ramparts were built

Ramparts at Stanwick, reinforced with a wall, enclosed an area nearly four miles long

around the original settlement. Excavation here has revealed timber roundhouses and other structures dating from the middle of the 1st century AD. Pottery and other finds show that during the reign of Cartimandua, the Brigantes at Stanwick enjoyed access to luxury goods imported from other areas of the Roman Empire. Excavated items include amphora jars for storing wine, ceramics from southern France and the Rhineland and German and Italian glass. As the site developed rapidly into an important trading post and a major centre of Brigantian power, the ramparts were extended. Although Stanwick flourished for several decades during the 1st century, it declined in importance after AD 70 when Roman power and influence expanded northwards. The present form of the earthworks owes much to landscaping carried out in the 18th century by the owners of Stanwick Hall and Forcett Hall.

The remains at Stanwick – once a stronghold of the powerful Brigantes tribe

On minor road off A6274, at Forcett village
OS Map 92, ref NZ 179124

Steeton Hall Gateway, flanked by a battlemented wall

4 miles NE of Castleford, on a minor road off A162 at South Milford
OS Map 105, ref SE 484314
Open 10am–5pm daily (exterior only)

History

Steeton Hall Gateway is one surviving element of a medieval manorial complex. The solar, or private apartment, and some later buildings also still exist, although the latter are on private land and are not open to the public. The manor of Steeton, originally called Stiveton, was held by the Reygate family from the mid-13th century. The gateway, which controlled the entrance to the manor house on the site of Steeton Hall, was probably built by William de Reygate, a royal administrator in the county of York. The two-storey gateway probably dates from about 1360, while the short lengths of battlemented wall are possibly of a later date. The manor eventually passed by marriage into the Foljambes family who held it for 300 years. The gatehouse was taken into state guardianship in 1948.

Description

The gateway can only be viewed externally. Visible from the road are two gate passages, a large one for vehicles and a smaller one for pedestrians. On the south side a stair turret with an internal spiral stair leads up to the first floor and roof. The short staircase on the opposite side of the gate passage leads to a porter's lodge; a small loop or window enabled the porter to see into the passage.

On the first floor a projecting chimney stack with an octagonal chimney is supported on four corbels with carved heads. Other corbels supporting the crenellated parapet are carved with heraldic devices of prominent families and individuals, including John Thoresby, Archbishop of York; the Harengills and the Reygates; and possibly the Malbis.

The path leading down from the car park overlooking Wharram Percy has been used since before Roman times. It was also the route taken on 26 June 1948 by Maurice Beresford, an energetic young economic historian at Leeds University. His visit to the puzzlingly isolated church was prompted by his quest to prove a much-disputed theory that massive depopulation had occurred in rural England from the Middle Ages onwards. What Beresford stumbled upon that day at Wharram – the buried and overgrown foundations of dozens of buildings strung out along sunken trackways, with a millpond surviving next to the dilapidated church – gave him good evidence for his theory about deserted villages.

Two years after his first visit, Beresford returned to Wharram to confirm his theory beyond any doubt. So began the Wharram Research Project, a 40-year campaign of survey, excavation and documentary research, eventually involving hundreds of volunteers from all over the world

working under the joint direction of Professor Beresford (as he later became) and Dr John Hurst. Research since 1948 has shown that there are about 3,000 deserted villages in Britain. Wharram is neither the largest nor the best-preserved example, yet owing to the long history of research on the site and the exceptional degree to which it is now understood, it remains the most significant such

The millpond and church at Wharram Percy

Facing page: Plan of Wharram Percy

Aerial view of the deserted village from the south

village, a site of international renown and importance.

The only roofed buildings at Wharram – the agricultural labourers' cottages – are 19th-century, though they incorporate the stone walls of a farm building constructed in the

1770s. The rest of the farmyard and the adjacent farmhouse were excavated and the outlines of the walls are now indicated by stone kerbs. The walls of the ruined church, now lacking plaster, exhibit a mixture of architectural elements and styles that testify to successive modifications of the building, as well as the changing fortunes of the village. Atmospheric though the ruin is, with the millpond beyond it, visitors are sometimes disappointed not to find obvious signs of medieval houses close by. To see the remains of these buildings it is necessary to climb onto the level plateau and examine the surface of the ground, just as Beresford did in 1948.

Overlooking the church are the reconstructed ground plans of three excavated buildings: these are medieval longhouses and barns dating to the late 13th to late 14th centuries, with doorways in opposite walls and central hearths. As visitors walk northwards along the plateau, back towards the car park, they will encounter similar rectangular features, in most cases shallow hollows defined by low banks. These are the overgrown wall-lines of medieval houses, as Beresford recognised, though they can be difficult to make out in summer when the sun is high and the grass is long.

On the evidence of the early excavations at Wharram, Beresford and Hurst initially inferred, from the flimsy construction of the stone walling, that medieval peasants' houses must have been lightweight, crude and probably in need of constant repair. Later excavations, however, revealed traces of 'crucks' – pairs of massive oak timbers forming arches that supported the weight of very substantial roofs. Similar crucks are still visible in slightly later buildings on the North York Moors. At a stroke, the picture of medieval peasant life was transformed: crucks implied much better-constructed buildings of higher quality.

At the northern end of the site, close to the perimeter hedge, is a cluster of buildings that Beresford interpreted,

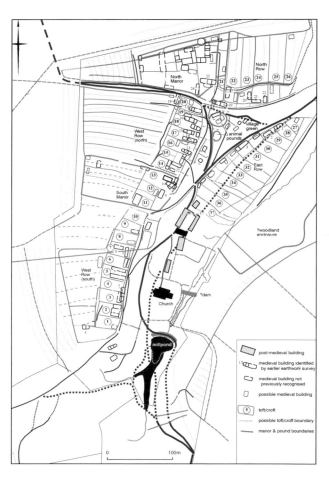

almost certainly correctly, as the site of the manor house built by the village's rich landlords, the Percy family. Distinctive features include the rectangular outline of the large barn, mentioned in 1368 as still standing, though the manor itself was reportedly already falling into disrepair. The circular outline of a dovecote, perhaps a 13th-century addition to the complex, can also be seen. The Percy manor house has never been excavated, but recent analysis of the surface remains suggests that the complex underwent a major expansion. This may have occurred in the 1250s, when the Percy family took over the interests of the Chamberlain family, who had, until then, controlled part of the village from a manor house closer to the church.

So why was the village deserted? It was long believed that the village had recovered to some extent after both William the Conqueror's 'harrying of the North' in 1069–70 and the Black Death in the 1340s, but that it must eventually have fallen

victim to long-term economic decline. It was the village's landlord, Baron Hilton, who was held responsible for finishing off the declining community, when, in about 1500, he evicted the last four farming families at Wharram and levelled their homes to make way for sheep pasture.

But the most recent research by English Heritage paints a rather different picture. Through analysis of the surface traces, it has proved possible to identify those last four households. It would appear that these houses and farms were bigger than those occupied by the earlier peasants, with access to larger arable fields and paddocks. Though small, it seems the community was not in decline, and may have been thriving. It is interesting to speculate what might have happened had Baron Hilton not opted for sheep pasture. Might Wharram Percy have survived in a shrunken form, like its neighbour, Wharram le Street, or would it even have increased in size once again, like nearby Thixendale?

Facing page:
Reconstruction of Wharram Percy village, showing the north manor in the late 13th to early 14th centuries

6 miles SE of Malton, on minor road from B1248; ½ mile S of Wharram le Street *OS Map 100, ref SE 859644*

History

The site at Wheeldale that is now in the care of English Heritage has long been considered to be part of a road that originally ran for approximately 40km (25 miles) over the Vale of Pickering and North York Moors. It was thought to be a Roman road, possibly linking a settlement at Malton with the coast near Goldsborough and skirting the forts at Cawthorn, south of Wheeldale. If it was an early Roman road, it might

View of the Roman road, looking south

have led to an unknown Roman fort; if 4th-century, it would have served the signal stations on the coast. Some recent studies question this, however, and suggest that the site at Wheeldale was a commercial route of a later date, or even part of an earlier, Neolithic boundary. Monuments of this type are very difficult to date because of the lack of associated archaeological finds.

Archaeological sites near to Wheeldale include late Iron Age or Roman square and rectilinear enclosures – which were most likely part of farmsteads – and cists, or burial chambers. One of these cists contained a skeleton, and these features may be of prehistoric date.

The first published reference to the site was in 1720 when it was described on a map published by John Warburton as 'Wades Causeway – Roman Way'. According to local legend, Wade was a giant who shaped the area by gouging out valleys with his bare hands. The site was also known as 'Auld Wife's Trod' in the

19th century. Since it was first described, sections of the stonework have disappeared. A length was re-used in the building of the modern road from Snape to Egton. Other stretches have been removed completely or re-used as foundations for enclosure walls. It was probably the lack of post-medieval enclosure on Wheeldale Moor that allowed this section to remain intact. The monument has been in state guardianship since 1912.

Description

The surviving section runs through wild, beautiful moorland, which is a Site of Special Scientific Interest, and it extends for just over a mile. It follows the western edge of a valley before dropping sharply into the valley bottom. It is constructed of large stones that are set into a sand and shale gravel mix, approximately 0.3–0.4m (1ft–1ft 4in.) deep. There is a top layer of sandstone slabs, which vary in size, with thin upright kerb stones on the north-east side. Its

Aerial view of Wheeldale Roman Road

width varies between 5.5m (18ft) and 6.5m (21ft). It has a camber with culverts running beneath it to assist drainage. Some culvert cover stones remain and several of the culverts have been rebuilt. The ditches on either side are probably modern. The section descending into Wheeldale Gill features a central rib of stone slabs which anchors the stone foundation. If the site was indeed a road, this rib could have provided traction on the steep slope.

S of Goathland,
W of A169,
7 miles S of
Whitby
OS Map 94,
ref SE 806977

The remains of Monk Bretton Priory, near Barnsley

History

The substantial ruins of Monk Bretton Priory, near Barnsley, are now edged by housing estates and industrial developments. When the monastery was built, however, the site in the wooded valley of the River Dearne was peaceful and remote. Founded in about 1154 by a local landowner, Adam Fitzswaine, it was a daughter house of the rich Cluniac priory at Pontefract. But within 50 years bitter quarrels – at times even involving gang warfare – had broken out between the two houses, as Pontefract sought to retain direct control of Monk Bretton. The dispute was only resolved in 1281, when Monk Bretton seceded from the Cluniac Order and became a Benedictine house.

The later history of Monk Bretton was, in comparison, uneventful. The priory owned properties across South Yorkshire, with rights over five parish churches, and worked coal and ironstone in the Barnsley area. In 1295 it housed 13 monks and a prior; there was exactly the same number at its closure in November 1538 during the Dissolution of the Monasteries.

After 1538 the priory was swiftly plundered for usable building materials: the north aisle of the church, for example, was dismantled and reconstructed as the parish church of Wentworth (though this was itself demolished in the late 18th century). The bells and church plate were taken to London and melted down. In 1589 the estate was bought by William Talbot, Earl of Shrewsbury, and the west range of the cloister was converted into a country house for his son Henry. The priory site changed hands several times over later centuries, before being placed in state guardianship in 1932.

Description

Little remains of the church, although there are several particularly fine examples of medieval grave slabs. Some of these still retain lead lettering set into the stone; others are decorated with beautifully incised crosses. The cloister buildings are better preserved. They include the high south wall of the monks' refectory, with its two great windows; parts of the chapterhouse; and the west range which is almost complete. This range shows extensive evidence of the conversion work undertaken in the 1580s. It was used as a residence until the late 19th century, which is how it survived.

Located beyond the cloister at the south-east corner of the site are the well-preserved drains that flushed the latrine block with running water brought from the River Dearne.

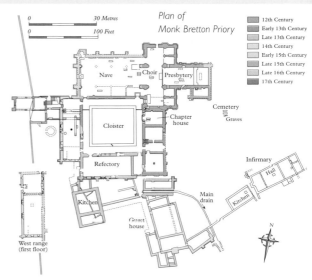

Plan of Monk Bretton Priory

North-east of the church a large building of the late 13th century stands alone. It retains its medieval double-ridged roof, and, inside, tall octagonal pillars support the upper storey. The building was probably the courthouse and administrative building for the management of the priory estates. The imposing priory gatehouse, which was built in the early 15th century, is still almost intact, although roofless.

1 mile E of Barnsley town centre, off A663 OS Map 111, ref SE 373065 Please call 01904 601901 for opening times.

Among the 3,000 or so deserted villages in England, Gainsthorpe is one of the most clearly visible and best preserved. It lies in a grassy paddock beside a lone farmhouse, and is half hidden between the Roman road of Ermine Street and an ancient ridgeway to the west, now the B1398. Former streets in the village survive as worn 'hollow ways'. Beside them are individual properties separated by low banks, with 'tofts' – frontage plots that once contained buildings and sunken yards – and garden 'crofts' stretching behind.

The layout of Gainsthorpe's streets and buildings, seen in this aerial view, looking west

Some features of this small medieval village have been obscured by later stone quarrying but much survives. The 30 or so buildings – which are mostly one- and two-roomed houses and barns – survive as low turf-covered foundations, many with doorways clearly visible. Some properties were later combined into larger units around courtyards, indicating partial desertion of the village and conversion from arable to sheep or cattle farming. The well-enclosed paddocks and the cattle-pond were also part of this shift to pastoral farming. The courtyard ranges in the south-west area are probably the remains of the manor homestead and its home farm, with a rectangular fish pond in the corner and the footings of two circular dovecotes similar to the one at Wharram Percy (see pp. 31–5).

The village has two distinct sections, each centred on an east–west street and linked by a third street. The northern part was probably a planned extension, taking in some of the earlier crofts and narrow cultivation strips in the arable fields.

In 1697 the antiquary Abraham de la Pryme noted 'the foundations of about two hundred buildings, and … three streets very fare'. His estimate seems rather generous, though much may since have been lost through ploughing and stone-quarrying. He was also told that further buildings, including a church, had once stood further south, though no trace of these survives. The field strips that once surrounded the village have also been erased by later ploughing.

As is often the case, the time of, and the reason for, desertion of the village are not known. Some nearby villages were subject to plague, soil erosion or sand blowing, and others to deliberate depopulation in the Tudor period, when villagers were forced out by landowners converting the land to more lucrative sheep pasture. It may be significant that the last documentary reference to

Low earthworks, showing the position of the village's buildings

Gainsthorpe being occupied is less than 50 years after the Black Death had ravaged the country in the 1340s. Quite what happened here remains a mystery. In de la Pryme's words:

> Tradition says that the town was, in days of yore, exceeding famous for robberys, and that nobody inhabited there but thieves: and that the countrey, having for a long while endur'd all their villanys, they at last, when they could suffer them no longer, riss [rose] with one consent, and pulled down the same about their ears. But I fancy the town was eaten up with time, poverty and pasturage.

On minor road
W of A15;
S of Hibaldstow;
5 miles SW
of Brigg (no
directional signs)
*OS Map 112,
ref SE 954011*

The Saxon tower of St Peter's, with its distinctive decoration of stone strips

St Peter's, Barton-upon-Humber, is one of the most thoroughly studied churches in England and its history can be traced over more than 1,000 years in the building and in the excavated finds displayed inside.

In a prime position on the east coast, beside the Humber, Saxon Barton was wide open to Viking raiders, traders and settlers. The settlers, originally pagan, soon adopted Christianity, helping to fuel a great boom in church building of which St Peter's was a part. The first Christian use of this site was in the late 9th century. The stone church visible today was first built in about 970, comprising a tall tower flanked by a baptistery and a chancel. It has distinctive Saxon features, such as the use of large stones for doors and windows and a series of vertical stone strips around the tower – a technique derived from timber-framed buildings, but here largely decorative. Some of the stone was re-used from Roman buildings and was probably transported by river from Yorkshire. There was room here for only a small congregation: the church was probably built to serve a major residence to the east, which was a forerunner of the present manor house.

Domesday Book records in 1086 a flourishing market town at Barton with its own church, presumably a reference to St Peter's. About this time the tower was heightened with a new belfry. This survives, but a large new Norman nave and chancel, revealed by excavations, were soon swept away by further rebuilding. First the nave was widened with aisles, and over the next four centuries, the chancel, aisles and entrance porches were all rebuilt, sometimes more than once, on an ever larger scale.

The various phases of building are evident in the different materials and styles of Gothic architecture. Notable features include the rare, early-14th-century Crucifixion window above a side altar and a series of carved portrait heads, grotesques and 'Green Men' among lush foliage. By the mid-16th century St Peter's had grown to six times the size of the original Saxon church, while nearby St Mary's (which was officially a chapel under St Peter's) matched it in size and in splendour. During the course of all these changes – which also included restorations in the Victorian era – the original tower survived intact. In 1819 this was the first building in England to be identified as Anglo-Saxon, by Thomas Rickman, the historian who defined the various styles of Saxon, Norman and Gothic architecture.

Modern Barton could not sustain two large churches and St Peter's became redundant in 1972, passing into the care of the state in 1978. Displays inside show the results of excavation and research undertaken here since then. Skeletal remains from 2,800 burials (about a quarter of those estimated to lie here) have yielded important information on early medical practice, as well as the history of diseases such as arthritis. Conservation here is a continuous process. In 1999 the eight bells were restored in time to ring in the Millennium, echoing those that were first rung in this tower more than 1,000 years before.

The interior of St Peter's Church

In Barton-upon-Humber
OS Map 112, ref TA 035219
Open
1–3pm daily

Facing page:
Thornton Abbey's gatehouse, one of the oldest brick buildings in England

Right: Carved figures of saints above the gatehouse doorway

The remains of Thornton Abbey are the finest in Lincolnshire. Founded in 1139, the abbey was one of the Augustinian Order's richest houses. Following the Dissolution of the Monasteries in 1539, it became a college of secular canons, part of Henry VIII's scheme for a system to replace the monasteries. This too was soon dissolved and the site was plundered for building materials. The 14th-century gatehouse, however, continued to be used as a residence after the Dissolution and survived intact.

The gatehouse is not only one of the largest in England but is also an important early example of brick architecture. Originally, its brickwork would have been rendered and limewashed to blend in with the stone. The life-sized statues of soldiers and 'others of trade and sciences' once

manning the battlements have long disappeared but weathered figures of saints still stand over the doorway; even the original carved timber inner doors survive. On the upper floor are two large chambers – one of which now houses a museum – and a maze of wall passages. The chambers were probably used as apartments for the abbot or his guests and for the abbot's treasury. The abbey's coffers would have been well protected here. At a time of increasing insecurity for monasteries, the abbot was licensed to improve the building's fortifications in 1382, the year after the Peasants' Revolt. With its turrets, moat and barbican, the gatehouse would have provided good protection against mobs or raiders. It is also a swaggering display of the monastic wealth and power that Henry VIII dismantled so

*Plan of
Thornton Abbey*

effectively during the 1530s. The foundations of the church and cloister ranges are visible but much more lies hidden beneath the turf. Still standing are parts of the church and the chapterhouse (built 1282–1308), with its elegant panelled decoration. Alongside is the parlour, a small vaulted chamber where monks were permitted to talk. Behind the stone wall leading towards the gatehouse was the inner court, containing the

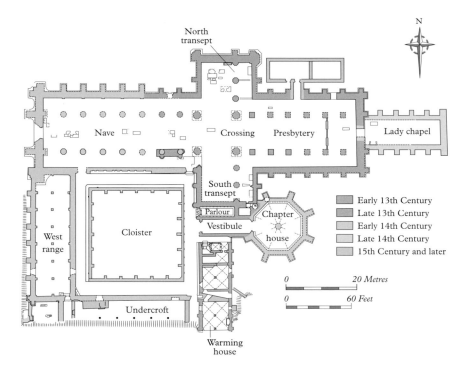

North transept

N

Nave   Crossing   Presbytery   Lady chapel

South transept

Parlour   Chapter house

Vestibule

West range   Cloister

Undercroft

Warming house

Early 13th Century
Late 13th Century
Early 14th Century
Late 14th Century
15th Century and later

0   20 Metres
0   60 Feet

brewhouse, bakehouse and other agricultural or industrial buildings.

The outer court, between the church and gatehouse, contained a watermill, stables, smithy and other service buildings. Here too is the overgrown site of a short-lived country house built in 1610, now marked by deep hollows where the stonework was later removed. In 1815 Lord Yarborough of nearby Brocklesby bought the abbey to protect it, and the site became a popular visitor attraction. In 1848 it gained its own railway station, which is close by. The 1850s saw some huge Temperance Society gatherings at Thornton, with up to 15,000 people coming here

from all over northern England for 'rational recreation'. Their verses celebrate the site:

> We will go to Thornton
> With speed upon the rail
> And there exclaim against strong drink
> In spirits wine and ale.
>
> Why we will go to Thornton
> And there we'll joyful sing
> Of liberty from alcohol,
> The potent tyrant King!

Left: Detail of carving on the chapterhouse
Below: The chapterhouse, built 1282–1308

18 miles NE of Scunthorpe, on a road N of A160; 7 miles SE of the Humber Bridge, on a road E of A1077
OS Map 113, ref TA 118189
Open
Abbey grounds:
10am–6pm daily
Gatehouse:
1 Apr–30 Sep: 12–6 pm, first and third Sun of the month;
1 Oct–31 Mar: 12–4pm, third Sun of the month

47

THE NORTH EAST

The history, landscape and architecture of the North East of England have been shaped for many centuries by the region's border status. Among the most significant monuments are those built by the Romans, in particular Hadrian's Wall. Although the Romans had conquered the Brigantes, the most powerful native tribe, by about AD 80, they were forced to consolidate their territorial gains.

Hadrian's Wall, stretching from the banks of the River Tyne to the Solway Firth and built in about AD 122, stood as the northernmost frontier of the empire for more than two centuries. By the end of the 6th century the area had been incorporated within the vast and powerful kingdom of Northumbria. In AD 637 King Oswald invited the Christian monks of Iona, led by St Aidan, to establish a priory on the island of Lindisfarne. Northumbria developed into one of the most important centres of Christian learning in Europe, with many other monastic foundations, such as those at Wearmouth, and at Jarrow in AD 681. St Paul's Monastery at Jarrow was home to the Venerable Bede, whose scholarly writings include the first history of the English.

Viking raids resulted in the decline of the kingdom and the abandonment of the monasteries in the 9th century. Following the Norman Conquest, however, work began in 1093 on a magnificent cathedral at Durham to house the shrine of St Cuthbert, Bishop of Lindisfarne, whose remains had been discovered miraculously undecayed in AD 698, 11 years after his

Left: The Bell Tower, Berwick
Facing page: St Cuthbert's Isle, Lindisfarne

death. The cathedral and castle at Durham became symbols of the formidable spiritual and secular authority of the Prince-Bishops of Durham. Their country residence was at Auckland Castle, refurbished in the 18th century in the Gothic Revival style, and its park provided with a fine deer house.

The medieval history of the North East is dominated by border conflict between England and Scotland from the 13th century to the union of the two kingdoms in 1707. The defences of existing structures built in intermittent times of peace, such as those at Bowes and Edlingham, were strengthened against possible attack. Other fortified buildings, in particular the bastle houses inhabited by Border chiefs and clans, are also characteristic of the northern landscape. The fortifications at Berwick-upon-Tweed, England's northernmost outpost, are among the most important 16th-century bastions in Europe. From the 17th century the North East was at the forefront of the Industrial Revolution, with its development was based largely on coal and iron. The need to transport raw materials led to major innovations in technology, most famously the railways pioneered by George Stephenson and Timothy Hackworth. Derwentcote furnace testifies to the Derwent Valley's status as the leading centre of British steel-making in the 18th century.

Hadrian's Wall: view from Steel Rigg looking east

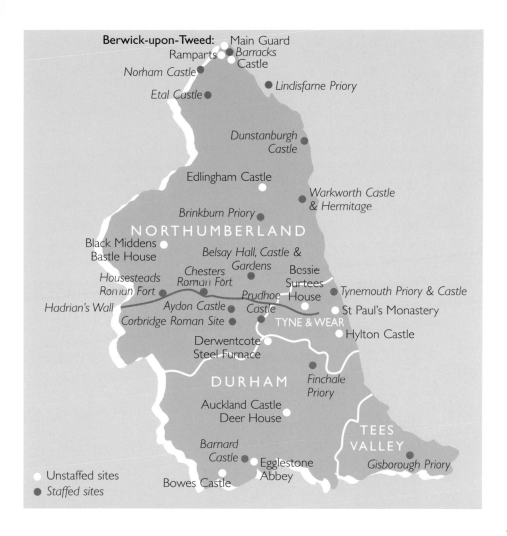

Berwick-upon-Tweed: Main Guard
Ramparts · *Barracks*
Castle

Norham Castle

Etal Castle

Lindisfarne Priory

Dunstanburgh Castle

Edlingham Castle

Warkworth Castle & Hermitage

Brinkburn Priory

NORTHUMBERLAND

Black Middens Bastle House

Belsay Hall, Castle & Gardens

Housesteads Roman Fort

Chesters Roman Fort

Bessie Surtees House

Tynemouth Priory & Castle

Hadrian's Wall

Aydon Castle · *Prudhoe Castle*

St Paul's Monastery

Corbridge Roman Site

TYNE & WEAR

Derwentcote Steel Furnace

Hylton Castle

DURHAM

Finchale Priory

Auckland Castle Deer House

TEES VALLEY

Barnard Castle

Egglestone Abbey

Gisborough Priory

Bowes Castle

○ Unstaffed sites
● *Staffed sites*

51

History

Auckland Castle Deer House is situated on a promontory within the former deer park of Auckland Castle. The Bishops of Durham have kept a residence at Auckland since the Norman period. Managed deer parks were an established element of rural life during the Middle Ages, as hunting was such an important part of the life of the aristocracy and nobility, clerical as well as lay. Shelters for deer were unusual. This much later example, dating from the 18th century, demonstrates that the deer park remained in use for several centuries. Built about 1760 by Richard Trevor, Bishop of Durham from 1752 to 1771, it provided a feeding place and shelter for the deer, and also had rooms in which the bishop and his guests could picnic, enjoy the views of the park and take a rest from hunting. As well as serving a practical purpose, it also acted as an 'eyecatcher', adding

Auckland Castle Deer House – a fine example of Gothic Revival architecture

The Bishop's Palace, Auckland Castle, with the Deercote Beyond, *by John Warwick Smith (1749–1831)*

interest to the view of the landscaped park from the castle.

Description

The deer house can be reached on foot from the castle through semi-wooded public parkland. The building is almost square, comprising a courtyard, where the deer were fed, surrounded by an arcade that was once roofed with slates. In the centre of the north side is an arched gateway, flanked by square pilasters, and on the south side is a two-storey tower, its first-floor room overlooking the interior. The building was probably designed by Thomas Wright who also produced designs for a gateway to the park in a similar style, though this was never built. The deer house is a rare and well-preserved example of 18th-century Gothic Revival architecture – a fanciful interpretation of medieval buildings – in the form of a mock castle with battlements, arrow loops, pinnacles and pointed arches. Parts of Auckland Castle were also refurbished in this style in the mid- to late 18th century.

In Auckland Park, Bishop Auckland; N of town centre on A68
OS Map 93, *ref NZ 216304*
Open
Park:
1 Apr–30 Sep: 10am–6pm daily;
1 Oct–28 Mar: 10am–4pm daily

53

BOWES CASTLE

History

Bowes Castle was built between 1171 and 1187 on the site of the Roman fort of Lavatris. The Roman fort can be traced for most of its perimeter. It was constructed to guard the strategic route known as the Stainmore Pass, and was occupied from the late 1st century AD to the late 4th century. The importance of this route and the crucial defensive position of the fort were recognised by Henry II who built the keep in the north-west sector of the fort. The castle was originally a possession of the Honour of Richmond but came into the ownership of the Crown when Earl Conan died without male heirs in 1171. King Henry II lost no time in strengthening a castle so vital for the defence of the kingdom against a Scottish invasion, which did in fact occur in 1173–4. Bowes was besieged by the army of King William of Scotland which immediately retreated when Geoffrey, Archbishop of York, approached with a relieving army. No further expenditure on its fabric is recorded after 1187, and, as the keep is the only part of the castle that still stands, the history of the rest is obscure.

The castle appears to have remained in Crown ownership until 1233, when it was presented by Henry III to the Duke of Brittany. In 1241 the castle and manor of Bowes were given to Peter of Savoy who was the king's uncle and also Earl of Richmond. Edward II subsequently granted the castle to John de Scargill in 1322, causing much local resentment,

Bowes Castle keep from the east, showing the raised entrance at first-floor level

and tenants of the earl besieged and captured the castle. After further changes of ownership the castle reverted to the Crown in 1471. By the 17th century it had become redundant, and after the Civil War parts of it were dismantled and the stone was re-used for other buildings.

Description

The castle now stands in a field surrounded by a moat on two sides. The keep is the only surviving part. It is rectangular in plan, with broad, flat buttresses at the corners and halfway along each wall. The keep was originally three storeys high. It was entered at first-floor level via a main door in the east wall, reached by a flight of stairs within a forebuilding that has now disappeared. The entrance to the building is now through an opening

that was originally an arrow slit. The two upper floors and the basement – which provided secure storage space – were linked by the spiral staircase in the thickness of the wall at the south-east corner. The first floor, suspended on vaulting added in the 13th or 14th century, was divided into a hall and a chamber by a cross-wall. Smaller rooms and passageways to latrines were constructed in the thickness of the walls. The north-east room was a kitchen. The spiral stair continued up to the second floor, now inaccessible and ruinous.

Outlet chutes for the latrines, visible in the west wall

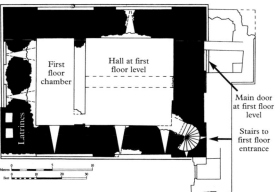

Plan of the keep of Bowes Castle

First floor chamber

Latrines

Hall at first floor level

Main door at first floor level

Stairs to first floor entrance

Metres 0   5   10
Feet 0   10   20   30

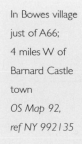

In Bowes village just of A66; 4 miles W of Barnard Castle town

OS Map 92, ref NY 992135

DERWENTCOTE STEEL FURNACE

The cone-shaped furnace at Derwentcote, flanked by sheds

History

Derwentcote Steel Furnace is the earliest and most complete steel-making furnace in Britain. It was probably built during the 1720s, as one of a series of steelworks along the River Derwent, at a time when the Derwent Valley and Tyneside produced about half of Britain's steel. The manufacturing process used at Derwentcote, known as cementation, had been introduced by William Bertram & Sons for the production of high-quality steel for springs and cutting tools. The steel was manufactured by allowing carbon from charcoal to diffuse into pure wrought iron at high temperatures. Near the base of the furnace were two stone chests, into which iron bars were loaded and then packed around with charcoal dust. The top was sealed with a layer of sand to prevent contamination by sulphur in the fumes from the burning coal. A cementation firing took about a week at a steady temperature of $1,100°C$. The furnace had to be left to cool completely for up to 10 days before being unloaded, after which the ashes were cleaned out ready for the next firing. The steel was then taken to a forge down the hill where it was again heated and then hammered to distribute the carbon content evenly. The furnace remained in use until the 1870s, although the cementation process was superseded in the 19th century by the Bessemer process which enabled steel to be produced more easily and cheaply. The Sheffield steel industry soon eclipsed that of the Derwent Valley and eventually the furnace fell into ruin.

Description

The building was made of local materials and consists of a circular cone-shaped furnace with sheds attached north and south. The roof tiles are modern replacements. In the larger, southern shed, or 'fessing house', stores of iron, coal and charcoal were housed and prepared for use. The northern shed protected the north side of the ash pit and ventilation shaft. The furnace is a

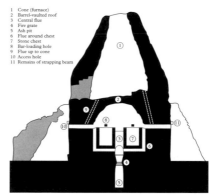

1 Cone (furnace)
2 Barrel-vaulted roof
3 Central flue
4 Fire grate
5 Ash pit
6 Flue around chest
7 Stone chest
8 Bar-loading hole
9 Flue up to cone
10 Access hole
11 Remains of strapping beam

Left: Section of the furnace interior

Below left: Inside the furnace

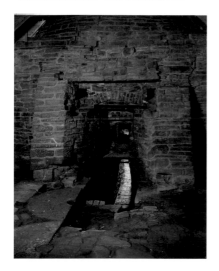

massive buttressed structure with a brick-vaulted chamber holding two coffin-like stone chests. In its thickness are a number of flues for heat circulation. A fire grate ran north–south underneath the cone, with steps at either end to the ash pit below it. Reddened stonework outside the cone and the glassy surface of the brickwork within were caused by the tremendous heat generated by the furnace. There is a small exhibition about steel-making, and Derwentcote itself, inside the building.

10 miles SW of Newcastle, on A694; between Rowland's Gill and Hamsterley
OS Map 88, ref NZ 130566
Please call 0191 269 1200 for opening times.

Although most of Yorkshire and the North East is still rural, industrial activity over many centuries has left an indelible mark on the landscape. The region's rich mineral resources have long been exploited. The extraction of alum, used in the leather tanning process and as a mordant to fix dyes, was among the most significant early industries. The Cholmley family of Whitby consolidated its fortune by working deposits along the cliffs in the 17th century. In the same area are some of the world's best jet deposits and in the 19th century Whitby became renowned for its jet carving. From Roman times millstone production was an

Above: Alum works depicted in The Costume of Yorkshire *(1885), by George Walker*

important industry on outcrops north of Sheffield. The Romans probably extracted lead in the north Pennines and by the 12th century the mining of lead and silver in Weardale was a well-organised industry controlled by the Bishops of Durham. In Tyneside, coal seams have been mined continuously since Roman times. Coals from Newcastle reached London, and even continental Europe, in regular shipments; by 1334 Newcastle had become the fourth richest town in England. In the Middle Ages bell-shaped mines were dug to extract coal lying near the surface. By the 18th century mine shafts were sunk deeper underground. To prevent flooding, more powerful pumps than the horse-driven 'gin-gans' were required. Steam engines were first developed in northern England to drive pumps and winding engines that brought up coal to the surface.

The development of the railways was another by-product of the growth of industry and many of the great pioneers, including William Hedley and George and Robert Stephenson, came from the region. The first railways, known as 'Newcastle Roads', used wooden rails along which the

THE INDUSTRIAL HERITAGE OF NORTHERN ENGLAND

coal carts were drawn by horse. They were later replaced by 'steam engines on wheels', or locomotives. In 1822 George Stephenson created a steam railway for Hetton Colliery. This served as a model for the world's first public railway, built between Stockton and Darlington in 1825. The new railways facilitated the expansion of mining in the Durham coalfield, and, from the 1830s, the development of new ports such as Middlesbrough, Sunderland and Hartlepool. Today, however, the railway network has shrunk and coal mining has almost disappeared in the area.

Further south, towns such as Rotherham, Barnsley and Sheffield grew rapidly in Victorian times, thanks to plentiful coal supplies and the new rail network. The reputation of Sheffield's cutlers stretches back to the 14th century – in Chaucer's *Canterbury Tales* the Miller carried a Sheffield 'thwitel', or long knife. The early iron industry in Sheffield used water power for forges, blast furnaces and rolling mills, although later ever-larger factories were built, powered by steam and electricity.

Sheffield saw many major industrial innovations, notably the invention of crucible, or cast, steel by Benjamin Huntsman in the late 18th century. In 1903 the manufacture of stainless steel was also pioneered in the city, by then the fourth largest in England. The metal trades are still active today, with new materials and products competing successfully on the world market.

The many Victorian factories and public buildings in the region's towns and cities display the pride, confidence and ambition of this age of rapid growth. Through partnerships, English Heritage provides grant aid and expertise to help preserve the region's surviving industrial heritage.

Above: Teapot and milk jug (1963–4), designed and made by the Sheffield silversmith David Mellor

Right: George Stephenson's Rocket *(1829)*

History

The abbey of St Mary and St John the Baptist was founded at Egglestone between 1195 and 1198 for Premonstratensian canons. St Norbert had founded the Premonstratensian Order at Prémontré in France in 1121, adopting the rule of St Augustine and borrowing from the stricter Cistercians' rule. The founders of Egglestone were the de Moulton family, whose title passed to the Dacres by marriage in 1314.

The endowment of Egglestone was so small that early in the 13th century the Abbot of Prémontré deputed three of his English abbots to hold an inquiry to decide if the status of the abbey should be reduced to that of a priory. It remained an abbey, but poverty beset the canons throughout their history. They suffered particularly when the Scots ravaged Yorkshire in 1315 and at other times of war, receiving frequent remissions of taxes to maintain them.

After the Dissolution of the Monasteries, the site was granted to Robert Strelley in 1548. He converted the east and north ranges into a mansion and installed a kitchen in the west range. In 1770 Sir Thomas Robinson sold the abbey to John

Egglestone Abbey from the north-east

Morritt of Rokeby Hall. Morritt's descendant placed the ruins in the guardianship of the state in 1925 and later returned a notable collection of architectural stonework, including the tomb of Sir Ralph Bowes of Streatlam (died 1482), which was re-erected in the church crossing.

Description

Egglestone is situated above the River Tees about a mile south-east of Barnard Castle (see p. 92). The abbey has a fairly unconventional plan, with its church on the south side of the cloister. The first church, built about 1200, was small and narrow, occupying only two-thirds the length of the cloister, but in about 1250 a larger presbytery with broad transepts was built, presumably to accommodate the altars required for an increased number of canons. Apart from the church and the east range, little else survives above ground.

The north and west walls of the nave are the only parts of the original church still standing; the nave was later widened southwards. The great eastern window of five lights consists, uniquely, of four tall mullions without any tracery. Under the crossing is the black stone table-tomb of Sir Ralph Bowes, but its top is missing. Many other tomb slabs are evident on site.

In the east range, the chapterhouse is next to the church. North of this the range was two storeys high, with the monks' dormitory on the first floor. Nearly all the monastic features of this range were swept away when it was converted into a house and later into farmworkers' dwellings. Beyond, a vaulted undercroft survives with a room above, adjoining the garderobe, or latrine.

The north range was built slightly later than the east. Its principal rooms were the first-floor refectory and the warming house (where the monks warmed themselves). The range was vaulted but is now ruined. The additional masonry near the west end of the north wall was the base for a fireplace that was added when Strelley converted the refectory into a hall.

Doorway into the nave in the south wall

1 mile S of Barnard Castle, on a minor road off B6277
OS Map 92, ref NZ 062151
Open 10am–6pm daily

BERWICK-UPON-TWEED CASTLE,

Situated at the mouth of the River Tweed near the border of two kingdoms, the town of Berwick suffered centuries of conflict, as control of the town passed back and forward between England and Scotland until the late 17th century. Each crisis brought repairs and improvements to the fortifications, culminating in the great

Aerial view showing the fortifications at Berwick-upon-Tweed

artillery ramparts begun in 1558. These survive largely intact and make Berwick one of the most important fortified towns of Europe.

History

The prosperous royal burgh of Berwick had been part of Scotland for more than three centuries when, in 1292, Edward I of England declared John de Balliol King of Scotland in Berwick Castle. Edward's feudal claims over Balliol soon led to Scottish discontent and to Scotland's alliance with France. English policy was to make war. Berwick was captured in 1296 but retaken by Robert Bruce in 1318. The town changed sides several times before finally being recaptured by the English in 1482.

High walls and flanking towers, like those built at Berwick, were normally sufficient security against

attack and damage from siege engines in the Middle Ages. But the development of gunpowder artillery in the 16th century slowly destroyed the value of traditional fortifications and it was not possible to adapt them satisfactorily. In western Europe an entirely new kind of artillery defence was developed, of which the Berwick ramparts are an outstanding example.

The north-east corner of the town was particularly vulnerable to attack and in 1539–42 a massive circular fortification was erected here, later called Lord's Mount. In Henry VIII's reign other works elsewhere around the walls were carried out.

The next development was the introduction of bastioned fortification, found first in Italy at Verona. In 1558 Mary I ordered the English military engineer Sir Richard Lee to Berwick to replace the medieval walls with a bastioned fortification system. In that year Calais had been lost to the French who urged the Scots to attack England's northern outpost. Bastions are gun emplacements projecting

from the wall, enabling defenders to fire outwards across the ditch, or alternatively to repel an enemy attacking the walls to either side. The construction of the new fortifications (which after Mary's death in 1558 became known as

Reconstruction drawing of Berwick Castle in about 1300

the Elizabethan ramparts) continued as fast as possible but stopped in 1569 before work on the upper ramparts had begun. By 1568, when Mary, Queen of Scots, fled to England, the Franco-Scottish threat had subsided. As it became clear that James VI of Scotland would succeed Elizabeth I as James I of England, no further work was done to the defences for the remainder of Elizabeth's reign.

The Elizabethan ramparts were modified in the 17th century and the alarm caused by the second Jacobite

Above: Coxon's Tower from the west

Facing page: Lord's Mount and the Bell Tower

Berwick Ramparts

Visitors should keep to the paths as there are steep hidden drops. Children should be closely supervised.

rising in 1745–6 ensured that they were kept in good order in the 18th century. During the Napoleonic Wars it was proposed to abandon those works that could not be used for the defence of the estuary. The end of Berwick as a fortified town is marked in the 19th century by the enlargement of Scotsgate, the removal of the Main Guard to the rear of Palace Green and, in 1837, the creation of the pedestrian way along the ramparts.

Description

It is possible to walk the entire circuit of the town fortifications; you may find it useful to follow a route clockwise from Meg's Mount or, following a visit to Berwick Barracks (see p. 93), from the Windmill Bastion. The walls of the Elizabethan ramparts, faced in grey limestone, stand about 6m (20ft) high. Above the walls the rampart

earthwork rises a further 5m (16ft). Outside there was a broad, deep ditch, or moat, that is now dry. On the other side there was originally a high retaining wall similar to that of the rampart.

Proceeding from Meg's Mount, notable elements of these fortifications include Cumberland Bastion, which is one of the earliest and best-preserved bastions dating largely from Elizabethan times (though the earthworks above it were constructed in 1639–53); Brass Bastion, defending the north-east corner of the town; Windmill Bastion, a large regular bastion similar to Cumberland; and the Powder Magazine, a gunpowder store surrounded by its own walled enclosure and built in 1749–50.

From King's Mount to Meg's Mount, the Elizabethan ramparts were never completed and instead the medieval walls and towers were repaired and modernised. Against the southern rampart is the Main Guard, a Georgian guardhouse that used to stand in Marygate but was moved to its present site in 1815. Now containing an exhibition on the history of Berwick, it once had a soldiers' room, a slightly more comfortable officers' room, and a prison cell for the detention of drunken soldiers, deserters, petty criminals and vagrants.

From Meg's Mount the riverside path leads to the site of Berwick Castle. First recorded in 1160, it was completely rebuilt by Edward I with a strong circuit of walls and an array of impressive buildings, including royal apartments, a great hall and a chapel. The northern part of the medieval

walls can be seen beside the eastern half of Northumberland Avenue. The Bell Tower is conspicuous by its height among the medieval ramparts here. This four-storey octagonal structure was built in 1577 as a watchtower and bell tower, on the foundations of a medieval building.

Lord's Mount, a great artillery fortification with walls nearly 6m (20ft) thick, was built at the north-east angle of the medieval defences. King Henry VIII, himself a student of fortification, took a personal interest in the drawing up of the plans of these defences (though unfortunately they have been lost). The lower floor survives, with six casemates for long swivel guns and living accommodation, including a kitchen with well and oven and a latrine. An upper floor containing the captain's apartments and the crowning parapet was demolished when the Elizabethan defences were begun.

Castle: Adjacent to Berwick-upon-Tweed railway station, W of town centre; also accessible from river bank
OS Map 75,
ref NT 993534

Main Guard:
Berwick town centre, on N bank of River Tweed
OS Map 75,
ref NU 000525

Ramparts:
Surrounding Berwick town, on N bank of River Tweed
OS Map 75,
ref NU 003530

Today, the magnificent coastline of Yorkshire and the North East draws visitors in their thousands; in earlier times invading armies set their sights on this shore. During centuries of conflict with the Scots, an attack on northern England from the sea was as real a threat as invasion by land. The Romans fortified the eastern end of Hadrian's Wall with the sizeable fort at Arbeia (South Shields). In the Middle Ages the castle at Berwick-upon-Tweed – England's northernmost town – was the first point of defence against Scottish incursions.

Further south the coastline is still marked by castles of great historical, architectural

Above: Craster harbour, with lobster pots in the foreground
Right: Fishing boats converted to storage huts at Lindisfarne

and strategic importance. Some, such as Bamburgh, are still in active use, while others – Tynemouth and Warkworth, for example – are conserved as atmospheric ruins in the guardianship of English Heritage. The defensive role of these structures does not lie solely in the distant past: Berwick became home to Britain's first purpose-built military barracks, begun in 1717. The towns of Whitby, Hartlepool and Scarborough were bombarded by the German navy in 1914, and Scarborough played a role as a secret listening post during the Second World War.

If the sea sometimes brought threats, it also offered a livelihood to many. The annual autumn migration of herring shoals brought a bounty to the fishing families of the region. Small fishing communities, such as that at Craster in Northumberland, were renowned for their delicious oak-smoked kippers. Though the stocks of herring have been depleted, smoking of

imported fish continues in the original 1850s smokehouses. Further south, Grimsby became the world's leading fishing port and the docks, with their magnificent landmark Victorian tower, are still busy processing fish and imported goods. As in Craster, the traditional fish-smoking industry still thrives there, with its distinctive multi-chimneyed smokehouses. At Hull, one of the leading ports in the United Kingdom, the fish docks are still thriving. Ports were also founded inland on the Humber, Ouse and Trent rivers, notably at Goole, established in the 1820s. The fame of Whitby at one time rested on whaling but it also has a place in history as the port where the explorer Captain James Cook was apprenticed to a shipowner and where his ship *Endeavour* was built.

Tourism has a long history on this coast and is still thriving. Scarborough became Britain's first seaside resort when, in 1626, a Mrs Tomyzin Farrer claimed to have discovered the medicinal qualities of the town's natural spring waters. Amenities were built to cater for the fashionable families who abandoned inland Harrogate for the coastal town, especially after the

1660s when doctors began to promote sea-bathing as a healthy pastime. Gentlemen were advised to bathe for five minutes before breakfast, while ladies entered the sea later in the day from the protection of bathing machines, introduced in Scarborough as early as 1735. Mass tourism arrived with the railways in the 1840s: the development of coastal resorts such as Filey, Bridlington and Cleethorpes was fostered by rail links to industrial towns inland. Piers, promenades and pleasure gardens were constructed all down the coast from South Shields to Skegness, each resort catering for its own distinctive clientele.

Visitors on Scarborough beach, in a painting by T. Ramsay (c 1776)

BLACK MIDDENS BASTLE HOUSE

External steps providing access to the living accommodation

History

Black Middens Bastle House is situated in an isolated spot on the north side of the Tarset Valley. A bastle house is a type of fortified, or defensible, farmhouse peculiar to the Border country between England and Scotland. Most examples were built from the mid-16th to the mid-17th centuries, in response to cross-border raids and national boundary disputes. They are generally two-storey buildings, with living accommodation on the first floor and shelter for cattle and sheep on the ground floor. They were homes and refuges for rich freeholders, lairds and heads of Border clans. More prominent landowners had pele-towers, similar to bastles but with three or four storeys; most of these are found further south. Bastles were often built in clusters so that the inhabitants were within easy reach of their neighbours and could provide one another with support. The remains of a similar building (not in the care of English Heritage) stand nearby, while a mile away is a group of three bastles, all still roofed. Little is known of the history of this site and there appears to be only one surviving documentary reference to Black Middens, in 1583, when it seems to have come under attack in a raid by the Armstrong family. Many bastles were occupied until the 19th century, long after Border disturbances had ended. It is likely that Black Middens and the adjacent buildings were used as farmsteads into the 20th century.

Description

This bastle has several typical features. It is a rectangular building with thick walls built of roughly squared large stone blocks. As is usual, these are laid irregularly with smaller packing stones in between. Though the bastle house is now roofless, the lower ends of the timber roof-trusses are still visible. In 1970 it was recorded as having a slate roof. There was originally only one doorway, for livestock, in the east-facing wall. This has been blocked with masonry. The south wall has two modern doorways, inserted when the ground floor was divided by a partition wall; these are now blocked by iron grilles. For security the ground floor had narrow ventilation slits rather than windows. Access to the upper floor was by external steps and holes for a drawbar to secure the first-floor door can still be seen. There would also have been internal access, by ladder, to the living quarters. Some bastles had stone barrel vaults to support the first floor; others, such as Black Middens, had timber beams. At the west end of the upper floor are stone corbels and timber beam holes to support a hearth.

The bastle house from the east, showing a doorway for livestock, now blocked

180 m N of minor road, 7 miles NW of Bellingham; or along a minor road from A68
OS Map 80, ref NY 773900

69

EDLINGHAM CASTLE

History

Edlingham Castle dates mainly from the 14th century, although a manor house of the 13th century is probably concealed beneath the later building. The earliest standing remains are those of the hall house, built about in 1300 by Sir William Felton at a time when Northumberland was relatively peaceful. Felton was a member of an important family with estates in Norfolk and Shropshire but he had made his fortune independently through military service, royal favour and marriage to a Northumberland heiress, Constance de Pontrop. His successors made extensive improvements to the manor house. In about 1340–50 his son, also named William, improved domestic comfort by building a magnificent solar tower, the best preserved part of the castle. As the Anglo-Scottish wars continued, he also strengthened the defences with a gate tower and stone curtain wall. Towards the end of the 14th century William's grandson, John, completed the enclosure walls and enlarged the gatehouse. Later owners of the estate included the Hastings and Swinburne families. The Feltons had traditionally been royal officials and soldiers but their successors were primarily local gentry, with less need for military display or effective defence. The castle was abandoned as a dwelling in the mid-17th century and by the

View across the courtyard at Edlingham to the solar tower

1660s was being quarried for building stone. At the end of the 19th century only the tower was still visible amid grassy mounds. Since 1975 the remains have been in the guardianship and ownership of the state. They were excavated between 1978 and 1982.

Description

The castle is situated at the east end of the small village of Edlingham, on low-lying ground beside the Burn, a tributary of the Aln. The remains of the hall house are now mostly at foundation level. It stood on the south side of the courtyard and was a rectangular building with octagonal corner turrets. It would have had two storeys, with the undercroft, used for storage, at ground-floor level and, on the first floor, the public and private apartments of the lords of the manor of Edlingham. A curtain wall and gatehouse enclosed the hall and courtyard; only the bases of these structures now remain. The rampart that once surrounded the manor survives as an earthwork. A variety of service buildings evidently existed within the courtyard, including a kitchen, brewhouse and bakehouse. The foundations of the service buildings that are now visible date from the replanning of the courtyard ranges after 1514.

The best preserved part of the castle is the solar tower. This provided accommodation for the owner and his family. The north and west walls of the tower survive almost to full height; a forebuilding was situated on the north side and on the corners there were stepped buttresses, each originally surmounted by a circular turret with battlements. The tower is three storeys high and each floor contained a single chamber. The first-floor room has a double line of windows and the remains of an elaborate fireplace.

The solar tower – the most complete remaining part of the castle

At E end of Edlingham village, on minor road off B6341; 6 miles SW of Alnwick
OS Map 81, ref NU 116092

71

Below: Bessie Surtees House in an early 19th-century etching by Edward Richardson
Facing page: Engraving of the house

History

The two buildings now known as Bessie Surtees House stand on a stretch of Newcastle riverfront that has been used as a quayside since Roman times, when the first bridge

BESSIE SURTEES

was built over the Tyne. By the 16th century the commercial importance of the area was well established and many prominent merchants owned property here. The two buildings, originally numbers 41 and 44 Sandhill, were known respectively as Surtees House and Milbank House. Other houses further east along Sandhill are of a similar date.

The earliest reference to a house on the site of Surtees House is from 1465. The property was recorded as being owned by Robert Rhodes, a rich lawyer. Carvings on the fireplace in the principal first-floor room of the house record a wedding in 1657. The groom was Alexander Davison and the bride a daughter of Ralph Cock, mayor of Newcastle in 1634. The couple's family owned the house until 1770, when it was sold to Snow Clayton, a merchant. One of his tenants was Aubone Surtees, whose daughter Bessie is said to have eloped in 1772 from a first-floor window with John Scott, a coal merchant's son. They ran away to Scotland where

The window through which Bessie Surtees eloped with her lover, John Scott, later Lord Eldon

they were married (and were remarried in Newcastle after the families were reconciled). Scott eventually became a successful lawyer and, as Lord Eldon, Lord Chancellor of England. The site of Milbank House was occupied in the second half of the 15th century by Thomas Hanson. The ownership descended to Mark Milbank, who married Dorothy, another daughter of Ralph Cock. Milbank House was later also bought by Clayton.

From the late 18th century the richer merchants of Newcastle moved from the busy quayside to the more fashionable suburbs. The houses were divided up and let, and subsequently entered a period of slow decline. In 1930, however, they were bought by S R Vereker, later Lord Gort, a descendant of Lord and Lady Eldon. He employed an engineer, R F Wilkinson, to restore the houses using 17th-century architectural fittings salvaged from properties which were due to be demolished. Bessie Surtees House was bought from the Gort estate by Newcastle City Council in 1978 and leased to English Heritage in 1989. The rooms on the first floor are now open to visitors, while the rest of the building is used as offices.

Description

The buildings are rare examples of Jacobean domestic architecture, built towards the end of the timber-framing tradition. Both are five storeys high and had shops or stores at ground level with living accommodation above.

Milbank House was constructed in the 16th century but was refronted in red brick in the early 18th century. Its original timber-framed structure is now concealed behind a Georgian façade with elegant sash windows and shutters. Surtees House is a 17th-century structure with

over-hanging storeys above the ground floor. It has retained its original facade, featuring plasterwork decorated with classical details. The interior, in particular the principal room on the first floor, has fine carved oak panelling, elaborate plaster ceilings and carved fire surrounds.

Left: One of the firebacks on display in the house

Below left: Plasterwork and panelling in the principal first-floor room

41–44 Sandhill, Newcastle upon Tyne
OS Map 88, ref NZ 252638
Open
10 am–4 pm
Mon to Fri;
closed Bank Hols,
24 Dec–3 Jan
Tel: 0191 269 1200

75

Top: Hylton Castle

Below: The white hart of Richard II

History

Hylton Castle was built by Sir William Hylton as his principal residence in about 1400. The rich Hylton family had estates in Yorkshire, Durham and Northumberland and by the 13th century had assumed the title of a barony within the Bishopric of Durham. Hylton Castle was intended to reflect the family's status. Whether there were earlier buildings here is not known but the impressive gatehouse tower, the only part of the castle still standing, was almost certainly intended to be the dominant element of the new building. Other buildings were situated beyond the tower to the east, possibly arranged around a courtyard.

The Hyltons maintained their rank and wealth until the Civil War. Despite a reduction in their means, the family remained prosperous enough to refurbish the interior and add wings to the north and south side of the gatehouse in the first half of the 18th century. The last Hylton died in 1746 and shortly afterwards the estate was sold. A century later it was bought by a local man, William Briggs, who demolished the 18th-century wings, added larger windows and rebuilt the interior. The appearance of the 18th-century house is, however, known from a number of antiquarian illustrations. Further deterioration in the 20th century led to only the exterior walls being saved.

Description

The gatehouse tower, a substantial rectangular building, originally with four storeys, provided self-contained living accommodation for the Hylton family. The ground floor included a central gate-passage, which was flanked by vaulted chambers. Those on the north side were used as storerooms, while those on the south side functioned as the guardroom and as a private chamber.

On the next floor was the great hall, rising to roof level, with a kitchen, pantry and buttery at one end and a chamber at the other. Similar withdrawing chambers existed on the second floor; these were reached from the hall via a stair at the northern end of the projecting central east turret. The third private chamber on the second floor was over the kitchens and was reached via the main stair at the southern end of the central east turret. A further two private chambers existed in the central east tower, accessed via the main stair.

The principal features of the west front of the castle include four square turrets with projecting octagonal crowns. Carved figures stood on the

An engraving of Hylton Castle, 1728, by Samuel and Nathaniel Buck

battlements. Beneath the curved central support of the parapet and on the central turrets is a splendid display of heraldry featuring the arms of the king, the Hyltons and related families. On the east face are the arms of the castle's builder and the white hart of Richard II. One of the shields bears the 'stars and stripes' of the Washington family.

The large Gothic windows were added in the 19th century when William Briggs refurbished the building. Three courses of ashlar sandstone blocks are the only remains of the demolished 18th-century south wing; the north wing no longer survives. The ruined St Catherine's Chapel, founded about 1157, stands nearby in the grounds.

3³⁄₄ miles W of Sunderland
OS Map 88,
ref NZ 358588
(access to grounds only)

History

In AD 681, 10 monks and 12 novices from St Peter's Monastery, Monkwearmouth, were sent to Jarrow by St Benedict Biscop. They were to found a twin house to St Peter's on land granted by King Egfrith of Northumbria. The monastery was one of the earliest examples of Anglo-Saxon stone architecture in Northumbria. Much of the

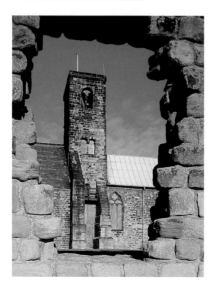

View of St Paul's, Jarrow, through the monastery ruins

construction work was carried out by continental craftsmen. The chancel of the present parish church is the only standing part of the earliest church, dedicated to St Paul in 685. The monastery flourished and became a major centre of learning in the north. Its reputation spread throughout Europe, chiefly because of the scholarly writings of the Venerable Bede who lived and worked here from 680 until his death in 735. He wrote more than 60 works, most notably the first history of the English.

At the end of the 8th century the monastery was sacked by Vikings and the community left. In the 12th century the establishment was refounded as a small Benedictine priory, dependent on Durham. The monks then dismantled the Saxon cloister buildings and restored the two churches. The medieval monastery prospered as a shrine to Bede and a place of pilgrimage. After the Dissolution of the Monasteries the eastern church remained in use as the parish church; the nave was partly rebuilt in the 18th century and was restored by Sir George Gilbert Scott in 1866. In 1783 the western of the two Saxon churches was largely demolished and replaced by a larger one. Although the community of Jarrow grew during the Industrial Revolution, much of the population moved away after the Depression of the 1930s, leaving the site isolated within an industrial setting. From 1963 the monastery has been excavated extensively, and it is now one of the best understood Anglo-Saxon sites in England.

Description

The nave of the parish church (not in the care of English Heritage) is on the site of the 7th-century basilica, remains of which can be viewed under the floor. The original basilica had no tower but was joined to the eastern church, now the chancel (built using much re-used Roman masonry), probably in the 8th century. High in the south wall of the chancel are three small Saxon windows, the central one with window glass – the oldest

in Britain – made in the monastery workshop and reinserted here after its discovery during the excavations outside. The excavations revealed evidence of two long buildings south of the church which have been identified as the hall and refectory of the Anglo-Saxon monastery. There was a later kitchen at right-angles to the refectory. Remains of a guesthouse, workshops and other buildings were also found towards the southern edge of the site.

All the standing masonry on the site within English Heritage guardianship is Norman or later. A refectory, planned for the Benedictine monastery, was never completed. The east wall of the west range still stands, preserving a triangular-headed doorway; the north wall of the south range, including the refectory and a fragment of its east wall survive. The ruins of a domestic building added in the 17th century are also visible.

The Venerable Bede writing in his study, in a 13th-century manuscript

In Jarrow, on minor road N of A185, follow signs for Bede's World
OS Map 88, ref NZ 339652

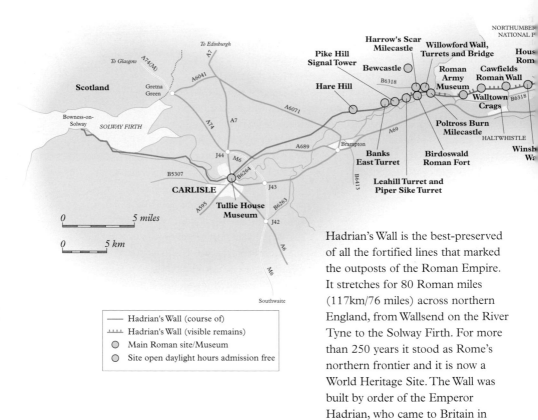

Scotland

To Glasgow

To Edinburgh

NORTHUMBER...
NATIONAL P...

Gretna
Green

Bowness-on-
Solway

SOLWAY FIRTH

Pike Hill
Signal Tower

Harrow's Scar
Milecastle

Willowford Wall,
Turrets and Bridge

Hous...
Rom...

Bewcastle

Hare Hill

Roman
Army
Museum

Cawfields
Roman Wall

Walltown
Crags

Poltross Burn
Milecastle

HALTWHISTLE

Winsh...
Wa...

Brampton

Banks
East Turret

Birdoswald
Roman Fort

Leahill Turret and
Piper Sike Turret

CARLISLE

Tullie House
Museum

Southwaite

0   5 miles

0   5 km

—— Hadrian's Wall (course of)

⊥⊥⊥ Hadrian's Wall (visible remains)

◯ Main Roman site/Museum

◯ Site open daylight hours admission free

Hadrian's Wall is the best-preserved
of all the fortified lines that marked
the outposts of the Roman Empire.
It stretches for 80 Roman miles
(117km/76 miles) across northern
England, from Wallsend on the River
Tyne to the Solway Firth. For more
than 250 years it stood as Rome's
northern frontier and it is now a
World Heritage Site. The Wall was
built by order of the Emperor
Hadrian, who came to Britain in

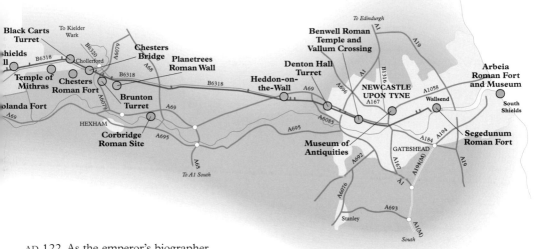

AD 122. As the emperor's biographer noted, the Wall was intended 'to separate the Romans and the barbarians'. It functioned as part of a larger system of border defences, much of which survives, including the remains of small forts a mile apart (known as milecastles), turrets and larger forts. Museums, visitor centres and reconstructions also provide a vivid insight into life along the Wall in Roman times.

For further information, please telephone 01434 322002 or visit the website at www.hadrians-wall.org.

A full-colour souvenir guide to Hadrian's Wall is available from the address given on page 84.

Information on the locations of sites along the Wall is given overleaf.

BANKS EAST TURRET
Managed by Cumbria County Council
On minor road E of Banks village; 3^{1}/$_{2}$ miles NE of Brampton *OS Map 86, ref NY 575647*

BENWELL ROMAN TEMPLE AND VALLUM CROSSING
Immediately S of A69, at Benwell in Broomridge Ave
OS Map 88, ref NZ 217647

BLACK CARTS TURRET
2 miles W of Chollerford on B6318
OS Map 87, ref NY 884713

BRUNTON TURRET
1/4 mile S of Low Brunton, off A6079
OS Map 87, ref NY 922698

CAWFIELDS ROMAN WALL
1^{1}/$_{4}$ mile N of Haltwhistle, off B6318
OS Map 87, ref NY 716667

CHESTERS BRIDGE ABUTMENT
^{1}/$_{2}$ mile S of Low Brunton, on A6079
OS Map 87, ref NY 914701

DENTON HALL TURRET
4 miles W of Newcastle-upon-Tyne city centre, on A69 *OS Map 88, ref NZ 198655*

HARE HILL
Managed by Cumbria County Council
^{3}/$_{4}$ mile NE of Lanercost *OS Map 86, ref NY 564646*

HARROW'S SCAR MILECASTLE
^{1}/$_{4}$ mile E of Birdoswald, on minor road off B6318
OS Map 86, ref NY 620664

HEDDON-ON-THE-WALL
Immediately E of Heddon village, S of A69
OS Map 88, ref NZ 137669

LEAHILL TURRET AND PIPER SIKE TURRET
Managed by Cumbria County Council
On minor road 2 miles W of Birdoswald Fort
OS Map 86, ref NY 586652

PIKE HILL SIGNAL TOWER
Managed by Cumbria County Council
On minor road E of Banks village
OS Map 86, ref NY 577648

PLANETREES ROMAN WALL
1 mile SE of Chollerford on B6318
OS Map 87, ref NY 929696

POLTROSS BURN MILECASTLE
Managed by Cumbria County Council
Immediately SW of Gilsland village, by old railway station
OS Map 86, ref NY 634662

SEWINGSHIELDS WALL
N of B6318, 1^{1}/$_{2}$ miles E of Housesteads Fort
OS Map 87, ref NY 805702

TEMPLE OF MITHRAS, CARRAWBURGH
3^{3}/$_{4}$ miles W of Chollerford, on B6318
OS Map 87, ref NY 859711

WALLTOWN CRAGS
1 mile NE of Greenhead, off B6318
OS Map 87, ref NY 674663

WILLOWFORD WALL, TURRETS AND BRIDGE

W of minor road, ³/₄ mile W of Gilsland
OS Map 86, ref NY 627664

WINSHIELDS WALL

W of Steel Rigg car park, on minor road off B6318
OS Map 87, ref NY 742676

The following sites along Hadrian's Wall charge an admission fee:

BIRDOSWALD ROMAN FORT

Birdoswald Roman Fort is set in one of the most picturesque locations on Hadrian's Wall, high above the River Irthing. Recent excavations at the site have uncovered a basilica, granary buildings and the west gate to the fort.
Please telephone for admission prices and opening times: 01697 747602.
2³/₄ miles W of Greenhead, off B6318
OS Map 86, ref NY 615663

CHESTERS ROMAN FORT

Set among the ancient wooded valleys of Northumberland, the fort at Chesters is the best preserved example of a Roman cavalry fort in Britain. It was one of a series of permanent troop bases added to Hadrian's Wall soon after the Wall was built and seems to have been occupied for nearly three centuries.
Open year-round. Please telephone for admission prices and opening times: 01434 681379.
1¹/₄ mile W of Chollerford, on B6318
OS Map 87, ref NY 912702

CORBRIDGE ROMAN SITE

The Roman site at Corbridge was strategically placed at an intersection with one of the principal routes into Scotland. Lying south of Hadrian's Wall, it was the site of a series of military forts and later a garrison town that flourished until the 5th century.
Open year-round. Please telephone for admission prices and opening times: 01434 632349.
¹/₂ mile NW of Corbridge, on minor road, then signposted   *OS Map 87, ref NY 982648*

HOUSESTEADS ROMAN FORT

Housesteads is the most complete example of a Roman fort to be seen in Britain. Occupying a commanding position on the exposed Whin Sill escarpment, it was one of 12 permanent forts added to the Wall in about AD 124 and was designed to hold a garrison of 800 soldiers.
Owned by the National Trust, in the care of English Heritage.
Open year-round. Please telephone for admission prices and opening times: 01434 344363.
2³/₄ miles NE of Bardon Mill, on B6318
OS Map 87, ref NY 790688

VINDOLANDA FORT

A fort and well excavated civil settlement. Owned and managed by Vindolanda Charitable Trust.
Open year-round. Please telephone for admission prices and opening times: 01434 344277.
1¹/₄ mile SE of Twice Brewed, on minor road off B6318
OS Map 87, ref NY 771664

Sixteen English Heritage sites in Yorkshire and fourteen in the North East are staffed. Most have a separate guidebook, which can be purchased at the site's gift shop or through mail order. These sites charge an admission fee, although admission is free to members of English Heritage (see inside back cover). Please note that sites listed here as opening 1 April open for Easter if it is earlier. Full details of admission charges, access and opening times for all English Heritage sites are given in the *English Heritage Members' and Visitors' Handbook* and on our website (www.english-heritage.org.uk).

Details of English Heritage publications can be found in the *Publishing Catalogue*. To obtain a free copy of the catalogue, and to order English Heritage publications, please contact:

English Heritage Postal Sales,
c/o Gillards, Trident Works,
Temple Cloud, Bristol BS39 5AZ

Tel: 01761 452966 Fax: 01761 453408
E-mail: ehsales@gillards.com

ALDBOROUGH ROMAN SITE
NORTH YORKSHIRE

Aldborough is the site of one of the northernmost urban centres of Rome's empire. Founded in the 2nd century AD, it was the principal town (Isurium Brigantium) of the Brigantes, whose earlier stronghold can be seen at Stanwick (see pp. 28–9).

Open 1 Apr–30 Sep. Please call for admission prices and opening times: 01423 322768.

In Aldborough, on a minor road off B6265.
OS Map 99, ref SE 405662.

BRODSWORTH HALL AND GARDENS

Brodsworth Hall is an outstanding example of a Victorian country house. It was built and furnished between 1861 and 1863 by Charles Sabine Augustus Thellusson and has survived with most of its original contents. The gardens have been substantially restored to their 19th-century appearance.

Please call for admission prices and opening times: 01302 722598.

In Brodsworth, 5 miles NW of Doncaster off A635 Barnsley Road.
OS Map 111, ref SE 506070.

BYLAND ABBEY

The abbey of Byland, an outstanding example of early Gothic architecture, was in its heyday one of the three great northern monasteries, alongside Rievaulx and Fountains. The remains of its large cloister and church reflect the size of the community that once lived here.

Open 1 Apr–30 Sep. Please call for admission prices and opening times. 01347 868614

2 miles S of A170, between Thirsk and Helmsley; near Coxwold village.
OS Map 100, ref SE 549789.

CLIFFORD'S TOWER
NORTH YORKSHIRE

In 1068 William the Conqueror built a castle on the present site of Clifford's Tower in York to strengthen his military presence in northern England. The tower is the most prominent remaining part of the castle and was rebuilt in stone in the 13th century.

Open year-round. Please call for admission prices and opening times: 01904 646940.

In Tower Street, York. *OS Map 105, ref SE 605515.*

CONISBROUGH CASTLE
SOUTH YORKSHIRE

The keep of this 12th-century castle was one of the inspirations for Sir Walter Scott's classic novel *Ivanhoe.*

Managed by the Ivanhoe Trust. **Open** year-round. Please call for admission prices and opening times: 01709 863329.

Located NE of Conisbrough town centre off A630. *OS Map 111, ref SK 515989.*

FOUNTAINS ABBEY
NORTH YORKSHIRE

The Fountains Abbey and Studley Royal Estate is a World Heritage Site that combines architecture and landscape of outstanding historical and aesthetic importance. The ruins of the Cistercian abbey, founded in 1132, are the largest such remains in Europe and provide a focal point for the landscape garden, laid out in the 18th century.

Open year-round. Please call for admission prices and opening times: 01765 608888. Fountains Abbey is owned and managed by the National Trust, with whom EH works in partnership.

4 miles W of Ripon, off B6265.
OS Map 99, ref SE 275683.

HELMSLEY CASTLE
NORTH YORKSHIRE

The spectacular ruins of Helmsley Castle, surrounded by huge ramparts, are set on a rocky outcrop overlooking the River Rye. Built in the early 12th century, the castle was strengthened and modernised throughout the Middle Ages. In the 16th century the west range of medieval buildings was converted into a fashionable residence.

Open year-round. Please call for admission prices and opening times: 01439 770442.

Near Helmsley town centre.
OS Map 100, ref SE 611836.

KIRKHAM PRIORY
NORTH YORKSHIRE

These striking ruins of an Augustinian priory are set in the peaceful Derwent Valley,

an area of outstanding natural beauty. The extensive remains include a 13th-century gatehouse with elaborately carved heraldry.

Open 1 Apr–31 Oct. Please call for admission prices and opening times: 01653 618768.

5 miles SW of Malton, on a minor road off A64. *OS Map 100, ref SE 736658.*

MIDDLEHAM CASTLE

NORTH YORKSHIRE

The core of the present Middleham Castle was erected in the late 12th century and was later adapted by the Neville family as a great residence in the 15th century. The castle is most closely associated with Richard III who reigned from 1483 to 1485. As a young man he spent several years at the castle and he later preferred it over his other possessions.

Open year-round. Please call for admission prices and opening times: 01969 623899.

At Middleham, 2 miles S of Leyburn on A6108. *OS Map 99, ref SE 127876.*

MOUNT GRACE PRIORY

NORTH YORKSHIRE

Founded in 1398, Mount Grace Priory is the best preserved of the 10 Carthusian monasteries in England. A reconstructed monk's cell and herb garden provide visitors with a glimpse into the lives of the medieval residents.

Open year-round. Please call for admission prices and opening times: 01609 883494. Owned by the National Trust, maintained and managed by English Heritage.

12 miles N of Thirsk; 6 miles NE of Northallerton, on A19. *OS Map 99, ref SE 449985.*

PICKERING CASTLE

NORTH YORKSHIRE

Pickering is a fine example of a motte-and-bailey castle, first built in earth and timber by William the Conqueror in the years following the Norman Conquest. It was rebuilt in stone and extended by later monarchs, notably Henry III and Edward II.

Open 1 Apr–31 Oct. Please call for admission prices and opening times: 01751 474989.

In Pickering, 15 miles SW of Scarborough. *OS Map 100, ref SE 799845.*

RICHMOND CASTLE

NORTH YORKSHIRE

Richmond Castle, overlooking the River Swale, was probably established in the 1070s by Alan Rufus to defend his northern estates from the Anglo-Saxon nobility dispossessed after the Norman Conquest. The castle subsequently developed as the centre of the Honour of Richmond, a vast estate spreading over eight counties.

Open year-round. Please call for admission prices and opening times: 01748 822493.

In Richmond. *OS Map 92, ref NZ 172007.*

ROCHE ABBEY
SOUTH YORKSHIRE

The remains of Roche Abbey, founded in 1147, rank in importance with the finest early Gothic architecture in the north. The transepts of the church still survive to their original height and stand within a dramatic valley setting landscaped by 'Capability' Brown.

Open 1 Apr–30 Sep. Please call for admission prices and opening times: 01709 812739.

1½ miles S of Maltby, off A634.
OS Map 111, ref SK 544898.

RIEVAULX ABBEY
NORTH YORKSHIRE

Rievaulx Abbey was the foremost Cistercian monastery in Britain. Much of what is now visible of the abbey dates to the mid-12th century and is associated with the rule of its third abbot, Aelred. The magnificent standing remains of the abbey church are a reminder of its original splendour.

Open year-round. Please call for admission prices and opening times: 01439 798228.

In Rievaulx; 2¼ miles W of Helmsley, on minor road off B1257.
OS Map 100, ref SE 577850.

SCARBOROUGH CASTLE
NORTH YORKSHIRE

Perched on a headland that rises high above the North Sea, Scarborough Castle occupies one of the most dramatic sites in the country. It played a prominent role in national events throughout the Middle Ages and Tudor period. A viewing platform now offers visitors magnificent views of the town and the Yorkshire coastline.

Open year-round. Please call for admission prices and opening times: 01723 372451.

Castle Road, E of Scarborough town centre.
OS Map 101, ref TA 050892.

WHITBY ABBEY
NORTH YORKSHIRE

A monastery was first established on the headland at Whitby in AD 657 and became one of the most important religious centres in the Anglo-Saxon world under the rule of St Hild. It was abandoned in the 9th century but after the Norman Conquest of 1066 a new community was founded. This grew into one of the richest monastic houses in Yorkshire.

Open year-round. Please call for admission prices and opening times: 01947 603568.

On cliff top, E of Whitby.
OS Map 94, ref NZ 903112.

AYDON CASTLE
NORTHUMBERLAND

Aydon Castle is one of the finest surviving examples of a late 13th-century manor house in England. In the 17th century it was converted into a farmhouse and it remained a family home until 1966.

Open 1 Apr–30 Sep. Please call for admission prices and opening times: 01434 632450.

1 mile NE of Corbridge, on minor road off B6321 or A68.
OS Map 87, ref NZ 001663.

BARNARD CASTLE
CO. DURHAM

Barnard Castle, high on a steep bank above the River Tees, is one of the great fortresses of northern England. It was built after the Norman Conquest by the Balliol family and became their principal residence. In the 17th century it was dismantled by Sir Henry Vane who used the stone to build parts of Raby Castle.

Open year-round. Please call for admission prices and opening times: 01833 638212.

In Barnard Castle town.
OS Map 92, ref NZ 049165.

BELSAY HALL, CASTLE AND GARDENS

Belsay Hall, Castle and Gardens form the nucleus of an estate that has belonged to the Middleton family since the 13th century. Until 1817 the family lived in the castle, a well-preserved medieval tower house to which a manor house was added in 1614, and from then until 1962 in Belsay Hall. In the magnificent garden, formal terraces lead into the wild woodland of the quarries.

BERWICK-UPON-TWEED BARRACKS

Berwick-upon-Tweed is one of the most important fortified towns in Europe, occupying a strategic position on the border between England and Scotland. The barracks, among the earliest to be purpose-built, were based on a design by the distinguished court architect Nicholas Hawksmoor. The barrack blocks now house various temporary and permanent exhibitions.

Open year-round. Please call for admission prices and opening times: 01661 881636.

In Belsay; 14 miles NW of Newcastle, on A696.
OS Map 88, ref NZ 086785.

Open year-round. Please call for admission prices and opening times: 01289 304493.

On the Parade, off Church Street in Berwick town centre.
OS Map 75, ref NU 001531.

BRINKBURN PRIORY
NORTHUMBERLAND

Brinkburn Priory was founded in 1135 as a house for Augustinian canons. Its church, begun about 50 years later, is the only complete surviving building of the monastery. Parts of the monastic buildings were adapted to form an elegant manor house, which remained a family home until 1953.

Open 1 Apr–30 Sep. Please call for admission prices and opening times: 01665 570628.

4¹/₂ miles SE of Rothbury, off B6344.
OS Map 81, ref NZ 116983.

DUNSTANBURGH CASTLE
NORTHUMBERLAND

The imposing ruins of Dunstanburgh Castle are set dramatically on a coastal headland. The castle was built on the grandest possible scale in the early 14th century by Thomas, Earl of Lancaster, and was much altered by John of Gaunt in the 1380s.

Open year-round. Please call for admission prices and opening times: 01665 576231. Owned by the National Trust; maintained and managed by EH.

8 miles NE of Alnwick; on footpaths from Craster or Embleton — 1½ miles of easy coastal walk.
OS Map 75, ref NU 257219.

ETAL CASTLE
NORTHUMBERLAND

Etal Castle was built in the early 14th century by Robert Manners, in a strategic position by a fort over the River Till.

In 1513 the castle was captured by the Scots during James IV's attempted invasion of England, just before the Battle of Flodden.

Open 1 Apr–30 Sep. Please call for admission prices and opening times: 01890 820332.

In Etal village, 10 miles SW of Berwick.
OS Map 74, ref NT 925393.

FINCHALE PRIORY
CO. DURHAM

The extensive ruins of Finchale Priory, dating from the 13th century, stand in a wooded setting by the River Wear. The monastery developed as a cell of the Benedictine priory of Durham Cathedral and until its suppressions it functioned as a retreat for the monks of Durham.

Open 1 Apr–30 Sep, Sat–Sun and bank holidays. Please call for admission prices and opening times: 0191 386 3828.

3 miles NE of Durham, on minor road off A167.
OS Map 88, ref NZ 296471.

CADW-WELSH HISTORIC MONUMENTS

95

GISBOROUGH PRIORY
REDCAR AND CLEVELAND

The east wall of the church at Gisborough – one of the earliest Augustinian houses in England – remains virtually intact.

Open year-round. Please call for admission prices and opening times: 01287 633801. Managed by Redcar and Cleveland Borough Council.

In Guisborough town, next to the parish church.
OS Map 94, ref NZ 617160.

LINDISFARNE PRIORY
NORTHUMBERLAND

Founded by St Aidan in 635, Lindisfarne Priory, on Holy Island, was one of the most important centres of Christianity in Anglo-Saxon England. It became a place of pilgrimage after the intact body of St Cuthbert, a former bishop, was exhumed in 698, 11 years after his burial. It was here that the famous Lindisfarne Gospels and other treasures were created by the monks in the 8th century.

Open year-round. Please call for admission prices and opening times: 01289 389200.

On Holy Island, only reached at low tide across causeway; tide tables at each end, or details from tourist information.
OS Map 75, ref U 126417.

NORHAM CASTLE
NORTHUMBERLAND

The huge bulk of Norham Castle, built in the early 12th century, withstood several sieges during its history as a military stronghold. In 1513, however, James IV of Scotland stormed Norham and destroyed much of it. It was substantially rebuilt in the 16th century.

Open I Apr–30 Sep, Sun–Mon and bank holidays. Please call for admission prices and opening times: 01289 382329.

In Norham village.
OS Map 74, ref NT 906476.

PRUDHOE CASTLE
NORTHUMBERLAND

Set on a wooded hillside, Prudhoe Castle commands a strategic crossing of the River Tyne. Built by the d'Umfraville family, barons of Prudhoe, it later passed to the Percy family, earls and later dukes of Northumberland. The castle successfully resisted sieges by the Scots in 1173 and 1175. In 1818 the ruinous medieval residential range was rebuilt as an attractive house for the Percys' steward.

Open I Apr–30 Sep. Please call for admission prices and opening times: 01661 833459.

In Prudhoe, on minor road off A695.
OS Map 88, ref NZ 091634.

WARKWORTH CASTLE AND HERMITAGE
NORTHUMBERLAND

Warkworth Castle is one of the most impressive castles in England. High above the River Coquet, its magnificent keep still dominates the castle and the village. It was home to the Percy family, the most powerful in the region.

Please call for admission prices and opening times: 01665 711423.

In Warkworth, 7½ miles S of Alnwick, on A1068. *OS Map 81, ref NU 247058.*

For information on sites along Hadrian's Wall, please see pages 80–83.

TYNEMOUTH PRIORY AND CASTLE
TYNE AND WEAR

The prominent headland commanding the northern approaches of the River Tyne has a long and varied history as both fortress and church. It has provided valuable defence through the centuries against threats from the Vikings, the Scots, Napoleon and, in the 20th century, Germany. The ornate remains of the 11th-century Benedictine priory can also be seen today.

Open year-round. Please call for admission prices and opening times: 0191 257 1090.

In Tynemouth, near North Pier. *OS Map 88, ref NZ 373694.*

INDEX

INDEX

FURTHER READING

Further information for most of the sites included in this book can be found in the English Heritage Conservation Statements. These documents, which are held in the National Monuments Record library (see inside back cover for contact details), outline approaches to understanding and managing the heritage significance of sites in English Heritage guardianship.

GENERAL

Breeze, D *Hadrian's Wall*. London: English Heritage, 2003

Pevsner, N *Northumberland* [*Buildings of England* series]. London: Penguin, 1992

Pevsner, N and Neave, D *Yorkshire: York and the East Riding* [*Buildings of England* series]. London: Penguin, 1995

Pevsner, N, Harris, J and Antram, N *Lincolnshire* [*Buildings of England* series]. London: Penguin, 1989

YORKSHIRE AND THE HUMBER

EAST RIDING OF YORKSHIRE

Burton Agnes Manor House

Allison, K J *A History of the County of York: East Riding*. London (Victoria County History), vol 2, 1974

Summerson, J *Architecture in Britain 1530–1830*. New Haven and London: Yale University Press, 1993

Wood, M *Burton Agnes Old Manor House*. London: HMSO, 1956 (1981 edition)

Howden Minster

Keeton, B *A Guide Book to Howden Minster*, 1996

Sharland, J S *The Collegiate Church of St Peter, Howden*, 1967

Skipsea Castle

Beresford, M *New Towns of the Middle Ages: Town Plantation in England, Wales and Gascony*. London: Lutterworth Press, 1967 (2nd edition, Stroud: Alan Sutton Publishing, 1988)

Butler, R 'Skipsea Brough'. *Archaeological Journal*, 141, 1984, pp. 45–6

Pounds, N J G *The Medieval Castle in England and Wales: A Social and Political History*. Cambridge: Cambridge University Press, 1990

Renn, D *Norman Castles in Britain*. London: John Baker, 1968

NORTH YORKSHIRE

Easby Abbey

Goodall, J *Richmond Castle and Easby Abbey*. London: English Heritage, 2001

Ryder, P *Medieval Buildings of Yorkshire*. Ashbourne: Moorland Publishing, 1982

Wenham, L P (ed), *The Dissolution of St Agatha's Abbey, Easby, 1536*. North Yorkshire County Record Office, 1989

Marmion Tower

Chandler, J *John Leland's Itinerary: Travels in Tudor England*. Stroud: Alan Sutton Publishing, 1993

Emery, A *Greater Medieval Houses of England and Wales, 1300–1500*, vol. 1 (Northern England). Cambridge: Cambridge University Press, 1996

Piercebridge Roman Bridge

Bidwell, P T and Holbrook, N *Hadrian's Wall Bridges*. London: English Heritage, 1989

Fitzpatrick, A and Scott, P 'The Roman bridge at Piercebridge, Yorkshire–County Durham'. *Britannia*, vol 30, 1999, pp. 111–32

FURTHER READING

O'Connor, C *Roman Bridges*. Cambridge: Cambridge University Press, 1993

St Mary's Church, Studley Royal

Mordaunt Crook, J *William Burges and the High Victorian Dream*. London: John Murray, 1981

Spofforth Castle

Bunnett, R J A, Weaver, O J and Gilyard-Beer, R *Spofforth Castle, Yorkshire*. London: HMSO, 1965

Stanwick Iron Age Fortifications

Wheeler, R E M *The Stanwick Fortifications: North Riding of Yorkshire*. London: Society of Antiquaries of London, 1954

Three articles on excavations at Stanwick have also been published in *The Archaeological Journal*, vol 147, 1990 (1991), pp. 1–15, 16–36, 37–90

Steeton Hall Gateway

Kitson, S and Crossley, E W *Archaeological Journal*, 21, 1911, pp. 203–11

Wharram Percy Deserted Medieval Village

Beresford, M and Hurst, J *The English Heritage Book of Wharram Percy*. London: English Heritage, 1990

Oswald, A *Wharram Percy Deserted Medieval Village, North Yorkshire: Archaeological Investigation and Survey* [English Heritage report, available in NMR]

Wrathmell, S *Wharram Percy Deserted Medieval Village*. London: English Heritage, 1996

Wheeldale Roman Road

Hayes, R H, Rutter, J G and Rimington, F C *Wade's Causeway: a Roman Road in North-East Yorkshire*. Scarborough and District Archaeological Society Research Report 4, 1964

Margary, I D *Roman Roads in Britain*. London: John Baker, 1967

Waites, B 'Monasteries and the wool trade in north and east Yorkshire during the 13th and 14th centuries'. *Yorkshire Archaeological Journal*, vol 52, 1980, pp. 111–21

SOUTH YORKSHIRE

Monk Bretton Priory

Booker, D *Monk Bretton Bygones*, 1993

Gilyard-Beer, R and Graham, R *Monk Bretton Priory*. London: English Heritage, 1966 (1983 reprint)

Hey, D *The Making of South Yorkshire*. Ashbourne: Moorland Publishing, 1979

NORTH LINCOLNSHIRE

Gainsthorpe Medieval Village

Leaky, K and Williams, D *North Lincolnshire: A Pictorial History*. Beverley: Hutton Press, 1996

Watkin, J R and Whitwell, J B *Changing Faces: Man in Humberside from the Stone Age to AD 1500*. Hull: Humberside County Council, 1987

St Peter's Church, Barton

Bryant, G F *The Early History of Barton-upon-Humber*. Barton WEA, 1994

Miller, K R *A Guide to St Peter's Church, Barton-upon-Humber*. London: English Heritage, 2000

Rodwell, W and Rodwell, K 'St Peter's Church, Barton-upon-Humber: excavation and structural study 1978–81', *Antiquaries Journal*, 62, 1982, pp. 283–315

Thornton Abbey and Gatehouse

Clapham, A and Baillie Reynolds, P K *Thornton Abbey, Lincolnshire*. London: HMSO, 1951

Coppack, G *The English Heritage Book of Abbeys and Priories*. London: Batsford, 1990

Coppack, G 'The precinct of Thornton Abbey, South Humberside: the planning of a major Augustinian house', *Land, People and Landscapes*, ed. D Tyszka, K Miller and G F Bryant, 1991, pp. 37–44

NORTH EAST

CO. DURHAM

Auckland Castle Deer House

Harris, E *Arbours and Grottos … with a Catalogue of Wright's Work ….* 1979

Bowes Castle

Kenyon, K *Barnard Castle, Bowes Castle and Egglestone Abbey*. London: English Heritage, 1999

Derwentcote Steel Furnace

Cranstone, D *Derwentcote Steel Furnace*. London: English Heritage, 1992

Cranstone, D *Derwentcote Steel Furnace: An Industrial Monument in County Durham*. Lancaster: Lancaster University Archaeological Unit, Lancaster Imprints 6, 1997

Egglestone Abbey

Colvin, H M *The White Canons in England*, 1951

Kenyon, K *Barnard Castle, Bowes Castle and Egglestone Abbey*. London: English Heritage, 1999

NORTHUMBERLAND

Berwick-upon-Tweed Castle, Main Guard and Ramparts

Clifton-Taylor, A *Six More English Towns*. London: BBC, 1981

Grove, D *Berwick Barracks and Fortifications*. London: English Heritage, 1999

MacIvor, I 'The Elizabethan fortifications of Berwick-upon-Tweed'. *Antiquaries Journal*, 45, 1965

Paterson, C 'The Bell Tower'. *Archaeologia Aeliana*, 28, 2000

Ryder, P 'The Cowport at Berwick'. *Archaeologia Aeliana*, 20, 1992, pp. 99–116

Black Middens Bastle House

Ramm, H G, McDowall, R W and Mercer, E *Shielings and Bastles*. London: HMSO, 1970

Edlingham Castle

Fairclough, G 'Edlingham Castle: the military and domestic development of a Northumbrian manor', *Château-Gaillard*, 9–10, 1982

Fairclough, G 'Edlingham Castle, an interim account of excavations, 1978–82', *Transactions of the Ancient Monuments Society*, vol 28, 1984, pp. 40–60

Fairclough, G 'Meaningful constructions – spatial and functional analysis of medieval buildings', *Antiquity*, vol 66, 1992, pp. 348–66

TYNE AND WEAR

Bessie Surtees House

Heslop, D, McCombie, G and Thomson, C 'Bessie Surtees House – two merchant houses in Sandhill, Newcastle-upon-Tyne'. *Archaeologia Aeliana*, 22, 1994 [available as offprint]

Polley, R *Bessie Surtees House*. London: English Heritage, 1997

Hylton Castle

Morley, B 'Hylton Castle'. *Archaeological Journal*, vol 133, 1976, pp. 118–34

Morley, B *Hylton Castle*. London: HMSO, 1979

Taylor, T *The Time Team Reports*. London: Channel 4 Television, 1995

St Paul's Monastery, Jarrow

The primary source is Bede's *History of the English Church and People* (written AD 731; available in

FURTHER READING AND WEBSITES

modern editions). Numerous other publications include the annual Jarrow lectures, which are on sale in the church.

FEATURES

A Marvellous Freedom

Jennings, B *Yorkshire Monasteries – Cloister, Land and People.* Otley: Smith Settle, 1999

Waites, B *Monasteries and Landscape in North East England: The Medieval Colonisation of the North York Moors.* Multum in Parvo, 1997

Writers and artists of Yorkshire and the North East

Beckwith, F *Yorkshire Historical Fiction: A Reader's Guide.* Clapham: Dalesman Publishing, 1947

Daitches, D and Flower, J *Literary Landscapes of the British Isles.* Harmondsworth: Penguin Books, 1979

One Great Workshop

Carr, G *Pit Women: Coal Communities in Northern England in the Early Twentieth Century.* Merlin Press, 2001

McCord, N and Thompson, R *The Northern Counties from AD 1000.* London: Longman, 1998

Simpson, D *The Millennium History of North East England.* Business Education Publishers, 1999

Wray, N, Hawkins, B and Giles, C *One Great Workshop: The Buildings of the Sheffield Metal Trades.* London: English Heritage, 2001

From Barracks to Bathing Machines

Barker, M *The Golden Age of the Yorkshire Coast.* Great Northern Books Ltd, 2002

Whiteman, R *Northumbria – English Border Country.* London: Weidenfeld & Nicolson, 1998

Useful websites relating to Yorkshire and the North East

GENERAL

www.english-heritage.org.uk
(English Heritage)

www.nationaltrust.org.uk
(National Trust)

www.britarch.ac.uk
(Council for British Archaeology)

YORKSHIRE AND THE HUMBER

www.eastriding.gov.uk
(East Riding of Yorkshire Council)

www.nelincs.gov.uk
(North East Lincolnshire Council)

www.northyorks.gov.uk
(North Yorkshire County Council)

www.visitthemoors.co.uk
(North York Moors National Park)

www.yorkshiredales.org.uk
(Yorkshire Dales National Park)

www.yorkshirevisitor.com
(Yorkshire Tourist Board)

NORTH EAST

www.bedesworld.co.uk
(Bede's World)

www.durham.gov.uk
(Durham County Council)

www.hadrians-wall.org
(Hadrian's Wall Tourism Partnership)

www.nnpa.org.uk
(Northumberland National Park)

www.northumberland.gov.uk
(Northumberland County Council)

www.visitnorthumbria.org.uk
(Northumbria Tourist Board)